Winning with AI - A practical AI strategy playbook for enterprises

Made with ❤ on the Notion Press Platform
www.notionpress.com

The diagrams are designed using napkin.ai.

With deepest gratitude, I thank my parents and the three guiding lights of my life—Aruna, Aadarsh and Abhitha. Your unwavering support, encouragement, and love have been the backbone of this journey.
— Balaji Venkateswaran

Scan this QR for companion website

Table of Contents

Introduction

Welcome to the world of AI strategy!

I have been learning AI, data science and machine-learning since 2013. Still learning. The field is ever expanding and there is no end to innovation in the subject. Things exploded in November 2022. ChatGPT and its friends came up and revolutionized the concept and existence of AI.

The buzzword AI is now everywhere. An AI-enabled sells a lot better than a normal application. Anything prefixed with AI can fly higher than any other technology.

Every enterprise has gone all out into bringing AI into their day-to-day work and processes. AI gives a competitive edge. Every business process which is repetitive, and manual can be automated using AI. There are two ways to bring in AI. One is by improving productivity of employees. Second is to improve and automate business processes.

The emergence of vibe coding tools, RAG for information retrieval and agents for execution of tasks are main drivers to bring AI into enterprises.

An AI strategy is the first step in bringing AI to an enterprise. The strategy tries to create a plan or blueprint to embed AI in business processes or help in productivity improvements.

For creating an AI strategy, there must be a data strategy. Every enterprise data source needs to be available, secure, standardized and governed. A set of compliance protocols needs to be applied to data before we decide on AI strategy.

Successful AI adoption does not begin with tools—it begins with strategy. An AI strategy sets the vision, boundaries, and roadmap for how artificial intelligence will be integrated into an organization. It aligns AI initiatives with business goals, identifies priority areas for implementation, and ensures sustainable outcomes over time.

As enterprises progress from POCs to large-scale deployments, the question shifts from *Can we do this with AI?* to *How do we do it responsibly and repeatedly?*.

AI at scale is no longer just a technology challenge; it is an organizational, cost and governance challenge. CXOs must think about risk, compliance, security, and ethics alongside innovation and speed.

Many organizations are realizing that models and tools are relatively easy to procure, but building robust, trustworthy, and sustainable AI capabilities is much harder.

There is a new form of cost arbitrage emerging, where the real savings do not come from shifting work to a lower-cost geography, but from combining powerful, low-cost model APIs with a smaller, higher-skilled team that can orchestrate them effectively.

I have seen and experienced firsthand that vibe coding is very powerful for simple applications and POCs. This can reduce the development/debugging and prototyping time for applications by 70-80%. Coding models are becoming more accurate and more reliable.

We will talk more about AI tools, prototyping, build-vs-buy, ROIs, vision, guardrails, cost, risk and compliance and several other topics in this book.

The are various frameworks and processes that can help in formulating an AI strategy for the enterprise. This book is my effort to help understand how to build a roadmap for AI implementation based on various factors and processes.

I have created a free companion tool at https://genmyaistrategy.com to help navigate the process of building an AI strategy from various requirements. Please give it a trial and share your feedback to balaji.venkateswaran@gmail.com for me to improve the tool.

Chapter 1 – AI & Business: The Strategic Context

Prior to November 2022, AI (and machine learning) meant recognizing faces on a group of photos, analyzing sentiment of text, predicting whether a transaction was fraudulent, recommending the next product to buy, or optimizing a supply chain forecast in the background of existing applications. Most of the use cases had some business impact, but businesses were not too keen to bring in AI to every process. The machine learning models didn't cater to Turning's test and were just helping businesses turn-around predictions from data into more revenue. Productivity improvement and intelligent process automation were still evolving.

Post November 2022, with generative AI, AI models are able to generate text, images and video. Generative AI can craft creative text and images; generate ideas and reason out on problems. These features can help businesses in their ways of working. The ChatGPT release revolutionized everyone's thoughts about AI. The augmentation with technologies on top of LLMs to work on enterprise data, perform tool calls and make coding easier meant a lot of changes in the way businesses work.

For instance, using generative AI, marketing teams can rapidly create and test multiple versions of campaign copy, visuals, and landing pages tailored to different customer segments, and then refine them in real time based on performance data.

In customer support, service teams can deploy AI assistants that draft responses to complex queries, summarize long winding email threads, and suggest next-best actions for agents, reducing handling time while improving consistency.

In software development, engineering teams can use AI coding copilots to debug and fix existing source code; create new applications in a jiffy and also build software for complex problems.

In HR, talent teams can generate tailored job descriptions, interview questions, and personalized onboarding materials for different roles, while also using AI to summarize candidate profiles and match them to open positions more accurately.

In finance and supply chain, analysts can ask natural-language questions of their data, generate scenario analyses and narrative reports automatically, and even simulate the impact of pricing, inventory, or demand shocks without building everything manually in spreadsheets.

The business aware of AI tools is just getting started. As businesses lookout for more tools, they find it easier to get their tasks done. Recently, tools like Claude *CoWork* and *OpenClaw* can help business perform analysis and automation without an application/engineering team and just complete their tasks using prompts.

	Tip: Before purchasing any AI tool or platform, write down the specific business problem you are trying to solve in one sentence. If you cannot state it clearly without mentioning the technology, you are not ready to invest yet.

AI should be seen as a tool to do things better and faster than as a replacement.

AI is more powerful when it can do things unimaginable by humans rather than just workflow automation.

All the drivers for using AI starts with defining an AI strategy.

AI strategy is a detailed plan by which an enterprise defines and decides where, why, and how to use AI to create business value, while managing the associated risks and changes. It is not a list of tools or a catalog of models but a coherent set of choices about which problems to solve, which capabilities to build, which investments to make, how to realize ROI and how to align people, processes, data, and technology so that AI becomes part of how the business operates and competes.

Usage of AI should become more outcome-focused, building and improving business value.

Instead of asking ***What can this model do?***; AI strategy will ask ***What are the most important decisions and workflows in our business, and how could AI improve them?***

AI strategy for an enterprise is a structured set of plans that defines how the enterprise will adopt, develop, deploy, embed, learn and govern AI to achieve specific business goals, derive values and stay competitive in the market.

Of course, there cannot be an AI strategy without a data strategy.

An AI strategy should not be applied to all business processes at once. The adoption requires a mindset change and selective enablement.

AI strategy formation focuses on (not limited to)

- Business Processes
- Organization culture
- Budget
- Talent
- Technology maturity
- Tools
- Data readiness
- Security and sanity of data
- Risk appetite

Also, current stats say that 85% of AI projects fail to reach production. The main reason has been due to improper or non-existent AI strategy.

The components driving an AI strategy are as shown below. We will delve into each of them throughout this book.

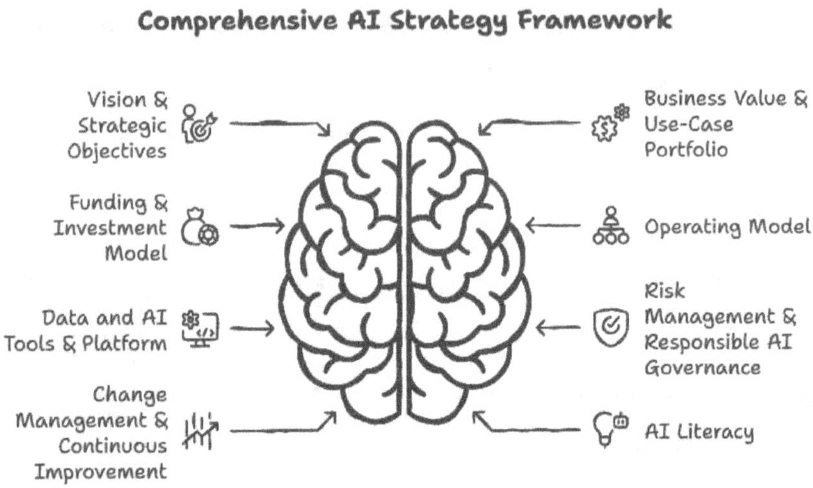

The strategy starts by assessing the maturity of an organization for AI adoption. The prioritization should be for ones where there are quick wins rather than a big bang huge adoption across the enterprise.

For instance, a hospital must try to adopt AI for administration automation and operationalization rather than patient diagnostics or clinical applications. In finance, customer service and agent productivity must be prioritized over credit line analysis and investment decisions.

We need to treat AI not as a buzzword, but as a very specific kind of strategy: a blueprint for how an organization will use AI to achieve its business goals, build durable capabilities, and manage risks over time.

It is the change from ambitious statements like "we want to be an AI-driven company" to have concrete decisions about where to invest, what to build, how to adapt an AI mindset and how to change the way people work.

Every AI strategy always starts with business, not with the technology. We should not start with what new AI can be used, but with "*Which decisions using AI define our success?*", "*Which processes are manual, repetitive, slow, costly, or error-prone?*", *and* "*Where could better predictions, recommendations, and automation change our revenue or customer experience?*"

In other words, AI strategy is rooted in value: it identifies the most important problems and opportunities in business and then deliberately matches AI capabilities to them.

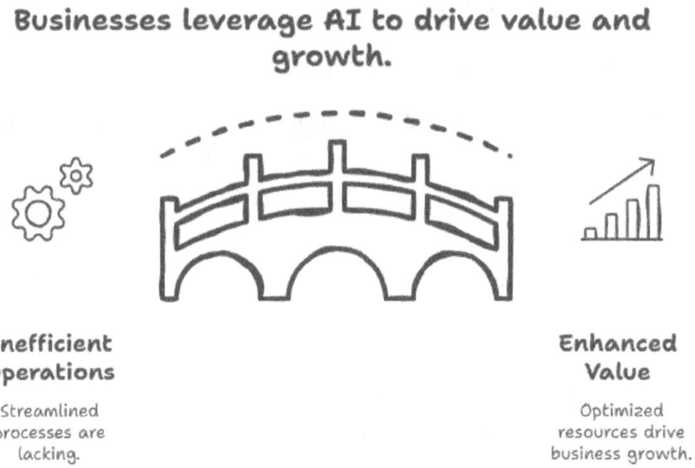

AI strategy is not simply a list of projects. It is also a plan for capability building. Every meaningful AI strategy initiative rests on three foundations: data, technology platforms, and people.

	Tip: Use my free companion tool at https://genmyaistrategy.com to generate an initial AI strategy outline before your first leadership workshop. It gives you a structured starting point rather than a blank page.

AI strategy and **data** are inseparable. A company that aspires to use AI for personalized customer experiences, for example, must first answer questions such as:

- ***Are customer records unified across systems?***
- ***Do we have reliable history of customer queries and feedback?***
- ***Are privacy preferences captured properly?***

Data is the key for success of any AI strategy. Data quality, integrated data sources and reliable data governance are essential parts of data strategy. However good or sophisticated models we might use for AI, without proper data and data strategy, AI projects are bound to fail.

AI strategy on the **technology** side tells the enterprise what kinds of AI capabilities it will use and how they will be delivered. This includes decisions about whether to use AI services from outside the company or build models in-house(**build vs buy** decision), whether to use a common platform for training and serving models, and how to set standards for how AI works with other apps. In the age of generative AI, this also means figuring out how to use large language models, how to connect them to internal knowledge (like using RAG), and how to safely put AI agents into workflows.

People and the way things work are both very important to AI strategy. AI changes who does what, how choices are made, and what skills are needed. A good AI strategy makes it clear how duties will be divided:

- Is there going to be a central AI or data science team?
- How will AI be implemented with the business, operations, and product units?
- Is it the technical team that builds an AI use case or the business team that uses it that owns its success?
- What are the new roles to be defined in the enterprise for AI strategy success?

AI product managers, data engineers, model owners, and domain champions must plan for training and change management. Without this, AI is just a technical curiosity and not a part of how the company works.

Governance and risk management are two other important parts of AI strategy. AI systems bring up new questions that old IT strategies didn't fully answer:

- How can we make sure that automated decisions are fair and easy to understand?(Explainable AI)
- When is it okay for a model to work on its own, and when does a person need to be involved? (Human in the loop)
- How do we keep sensitive information from getting into models that are outside of our control? (Data governance)

It should be understood that AI strategy is dynamic rather than static. AI is developing at 100x speed every month. The strategy has to align according to technologies, regulations, and competitive moves. AI strategies should be reviewed regularly, priorities refreshed, business values and ROIs monitored and failures documented with learning.

> *As an example, let us consider a regional bank that wants to come up with a plan for using AI. It starts by setting some strategic goals aligning with business, such as keeping customers longer, lowering operational costs, and making risk controls stronger. Based on these goals, it chooses the first AI use cases: a virtual assistant and internal agent to handle common customer questions and help staff, a system to flag high-risk transactions, and tools that help relationship managers get ready for client meetings by giving them*

> *AI-generated summaries and suggestions. The bank invests in bringing together customer data, setting up an AI platform in the cloud, and making a cross-functional team with people from IT, operations, risk, and front-line business units.*

> *Since the bank is dealing with sensitive customer data, there needs to be guardrails and governance. The AI decisions should be explainable and monitored on a regular basis. As the bank gets more experience, it adds more advanced personalization and new AI-enabled products to its strategy. It also updates its roadmap as new opportunities and challenges come up.*

To summarize, AI strategy is a plan, cultural and mindset change to achieve the benefits of AI across the business functions of an enterprise.

Chapter 2 – AI-maturity assessment

When we start to implement an AI strategy, the process has to start with assessing the current AI maturity level of the enterprise.

Similar to CMMI assessment for software development, AI maturity within an enterprise is calculated based on interviews with different personnel from the enterprise.

AI maturity assessment is a way to figure out how well an organization's AI capabilities match up with its strategic goals. It does this by finding gaps that can help shape the overall AI strategy.

Below, I have created a sample maturity questionnaire capturing various metrics for calculating a maturity score.

Instead of relying on a single self-reported score, the AI maturity assessment builds a snapshot of actual practice by asking people at different levels and functions — from executives setting strategy to engineers building systems to business users depending on them day to day.

The gap between what leadership believes is happening and what practitioners experience on the ground is often where the most important findings emerge.

The maturity assessment needs to be done periodically and the improvements captured. The score improvement is a measure of how well our AI strategy is working.

Each question in the list is answered based on the following scale:

AI Maturity level questionnaire answering scale

Score	Description	What it means
0	Not started	No AI activity
1	Ad hoc	Happens informally
2	Developing	Process exists but is incomplete
3	Defined	Process is documented
4	Managed	Process is measured

2.1 Data Collection

Answer these questions on a scale of 0-4(based on the meanings above).

Leadership and Strategy

1. Does the company have a written AI strategy that fits with its overall business goals?
2. Is there support from the C-suite or board of directors for AI governance?
3. Has the organization set a limit on how much AI it will and won't use?
4. Is AI investment tracked and reported as a separate line item, or is it hidden in the general technology budgets?
5. Do all the leaders in the organization know what AI it is using right now?

Governance

6. Is there a cross-functional AI governance body (like a council or committee) with clear members and decision-making powers?
7. Are the roles and responsibilities for overseeing AI clearly laid out? This includes who is in charge of the AI platform, privacy, security, and business unit accountability.
8. Is there a formal process for taking in new AI projects, and is it always followed?
9. Are the rules for AI governance written down, kept up to date, and easy for the teams that need to follow them to find?

10. How are the rules for AI governance enforced? Is it just policy, technical controls, or both?

AI Inventory

11. Does the company keep an up-to-date list of all the AI systems that are currently in use?
12. Does that list include not only systems built in the center, but also AI tools that business units have chosen to use on their own?
13. Is the inventory kept up to date, or is it just a snapshot that quickly becomes out of date?
14. Do you keep track of both third-party and built-in AI features in commercial software and systems you build yourself?
15. Is it easy for the organization to quickly find all AI systems that use a certain data source or work in a certain area?

Data and Privacy

16. Is it clear and documented that personal or regulated data is going into AI systems?
17. Do AI systems that use personal data need privacy impact assessments (or something similar) before they can go live?
18. Do AI systems follow the rules for accessing data? Can users only get information they are already allowed to see?
19. Are prompt and response logs seen as possibly sensitive data, and are there rules for keeping and accessing them?
20. Is the company keeping track of where data goes when it is sent to AI model providers outside of the company?

Security

21. Is the organization's standard application security testing program for AI apps?

22. Have AI systems been threat modeled, specifically looking at AI risks like prompt injection, data exfiltration, and model misuse?

23. Has the company done any red-teaming or adversarial testing on its AI systems?

24. Do vendor management include formal checks of the security postures of AI service providers?

25. Are there clear steps to take when an AI-related security incident happens?

Evaluation and Testing

26. Are there set minimum testing standards that an AI system must meet before it can be put into production?

27. Do you test functional correctness against sample use cases with known expected outputs?

28. Are AI systems tested for hallucination?

29. Are there acceptable levels of content safety and bias evaluations?

30. Are pre-deployment and post-deployment tests performed?

Deployment and Monitoring

31. Are there established criteria that AI systems must fulfill prior to their deployment?

32. Are AI systems monitored for operational health, including errors, latency, and availability, and are there alert mechanisms established?

33. Can you monitor an AI system evolves when model providers launch updated versions?

34. Are prompts and responses logged in a manner that facilitates compliance, debugging, and forensic analysis?

35. Is the organization capable of identifying unusual or potentially detrimental usage patterns in AI systems?

Agentic AI

36. Has the organization formally identified which of its AI systems possess autonomous capabilities, allowing them to perform actions rather than merely generating outputs?

37. Are the tools and APIs that agents are allowed to call clearly defined and limited?

38. Do agent actions that have important or permanent effects need to have human-in-the-loop checkpoints?

39. Are vector databases and agent memory stores considered sensitive data assets that need to be protected with the right access controls?

40. Are there protections in place to stop agents from going rogue, like getting stuck in infinite loops or doing things that lead to unintended consequences?

AI system Lifecycle Management

41. Are model versions and prompt configurations tracked for each production AI system?

42. How can changes be managed to see how model updates or prompt changes affect things?
43. Do AI feature rollback plans contain written plans like other important software?
44. Is there a formalized process for shutting down AI systems, including data cleanup, log retention, and user notification?
45. Are AI systems regularly checked for usefulness, health, and compliance?

Culture and Skills

46. Do AI system developers receive training on AI-specific ethics, privacy, and security?
47. Do business leaders who hire AI systems know project rules?
48. Can workers voice concerns about AI systems, and are they taken seriously?
49. Do company employees see governance as a way to responsibly use AI or as a problem?
50. Does it participate in regulatory forums, industry groups, or other groups to track AI governance changes?

2.2 Calculate Domain Scores

The 50 questions from the previous section are grouped into ten domains of five questions each. For each domain, the sum of question scores is used to calculate domain score (it is a percentage):

Domain Score = (Sum of question scores ÷ 20) × 100

Example: A domain with five questions scored 2, 3, 1, 3, 2 produces a total score of 11. Then, domain Score = (11 ÷ 20) × 100 = 55%.

2.3 Apply Domain Weights

Different domains carry different governance significance. Below weights are reasonable defaults for most large enterprises. They should be reviewed and agreed before scoring begins. And can be adjusted as per enterprise and business. But the weightage should not change in between assessments.

Domain	Default Weight	Rationale
Strategy and Leadership	10%	Enables everything else but is a lagging indicator of programme health
Governance Structures	15%	Core operating mechanism; without it, other controls cannot be sustained
Inventory and Visibility	10%	Foundational; no governance is possible without knowing what AI exists
Data and Privacy	15%	High regulatory exposure; typically the primary focus of external audits
Security	15%	Direct risk to the organisation, its customers, and its stakeholders
Evaluation and Testing	10%	Frequently underdeveloped; a strong signal of programme rigour

Deployment and Monitoring	10%	Operational continuity, incident detection, and response readiness
Agentic AI	5%	Emerging capability; weight should increase as adoption grows
Lifecycle Management	5%	Frequently neglected; critical for mature, compliant programmes
Culture and Skills	5%	Soft but foundational to sustained governance over time

The overall weighted score is calculated as follows:

$$\textbf{Overall Score} = \Sigma\ \textbf{(Domain Score} \times \textbf{Domain Weight)}$$

2.4 Mapping to Maturity Levels

The overall score can be mapped to the maturity level based on the bands. Most large enterprises conducting their first formal assessment are at Level 2 or Level 3. A Level 1 result needs critical attention.

Score Range	Level	Maturity Label	Characterisation
0 – 20%	1	Initial	AI use is uncontrolled and ungoverned; significant blind spots across all domains
21 – 40%	2	Developing	Governance exists in pockets; inconsistent adoption and enforcement across the organisation
41 – 60%	3	Defined	Core structures and policies are in place; meaningful gaps remain in depth and coverage

61 – 80%	4	Managed	Governance is systematic and measurable; continuous improvement is actively underway
81 – 100%	5	Optimising	Governance is embedded, adaptive, and benchmarked externally

2.5 Identify Priority Gaps

The overall score is a number. The real value of the assessment lies in gap identification. For each domain, calculate the shortfall from a target maturity level — typically Level 3 (60%) for enterprises establishing governance, or Level 4 (80%) for those seeking to mature an existing programme.

Domain Gap = Target Score − Actual Domain Score

Simply ranking domains by ascending gaps will give Year 1 priorities in your AI roadmap.

The domains with highest gaps are addressed first with an improved or adjusted AI strategy.

Some domain gaps may be due to the following reasons –

- Personal or regulated data is flowing to external AI providers without documentation or contractual controls.
- No privacy impact assessment process exists for AI systems handling personal data.
- AI applications are not included in any security testing programme.
- No inventory of AI systems in production exists or is maintained.

- Agentic systems are operating without human-in-the-loop controls on consequential or irreversible actions.

2.6 Worked Example

The following table illustrates a complete scoring calculation for a hypothetical enterprise. The enterprise scores at Level 3 (Defined) overall, with Agentic AI, Evaluation and Testing, and Lifecycle Management identified as priority remediation areas.

Domain	Raw Score	Max	% Score	Weight	Weighted
Strategy and Leadership	14	20	70%	10%	7.0%
Governance Structures	10	20	50%	15%	7.5%
Inventory and Visibility	8	20	40%	10%	4.0%
Data and Privacy	12	20	60%	15%	9.0%
Security	9	20	45%	15%	6.75%
Evaluation and Testing	7	20	35%	10%	3.5%
Deployment and Monitoring	11	20	55%	10%	5.5%
Agentic AI	4	20	20%	5%	1.0%
Lifecycle Management	6	20	30%	5%	1.5%
Culture and Skills	10	20	50%	5%	2.5%
OVERALL	—	—	—	100%	48.25%

Overall Score: 48.25% → Level 3: Defined

In the above example, the top 3 domains with largest gaps are Agentic AI, LCM and Eval. Our AI strategy and roadmap should address improving these first.

Tip: Treat the maturity score as a KPI, not a report. Track it over time and include it in executive dashboards alongside financial metrics. A rising score is concrete evidence that your AI governance investment is working — and regulators and boards increasingly expect to see this kind of structured evidence.

2.7 Reassessment Cadence

The assessment should be run on a defined schedule and/or after significant triggering events:

- Annually as a baseline to track programme progress.
- After any major new AI deployment or significant expansion of AI use.
- Following a material AI-related security or privacy incident.
- When significant new AI regulation comes into force in a jurisdiction where the organisation operates.

Tracking score changes over time is often more helpful than looking at one score. It proves to boards, regulators, and auditors that governance investments are working.

Chapter 3 – AI-First mindset

Ever since I started working in IT in 2000, there has been constant technological evolution. There was the dotcom era, mainframes, databases, cloud computing, mobile computing, digital transformation, big data and data analytics through the past 25 years. The recent AI evolution is the most disruptive one compared to anything else.

The new frontier is *AI-first* — not simply adopting an AI algorithm in pockets of work, but reimagining how the entire enterprise behaves when intelligence becomes native to every process, decision, and product.

An ***AI-first mindset*** means embedding AI into every process, activity, task, and department as a default approach.

An AI-first mindset is not about technology; it is about transformation. It reshapes how leaders think, how decisions are made, and how value is created.

In an AI-first enterprise, AI is not a department; it is the company's central nervous system. It runs through every department and team.

3.1 What It Really Means to Be AI-First

AI-first is indirectly data-first. Data has to be available and ready for making AI possible.

When a company is AI-first, it asks, ***How can intelligence, whether human or artificial, make this better?*** The question changes everything. AI-first companies design processes with intelligence from the start rather than adding AI later.

> **Tip**: Mandate personal AI tool usage before mandating enterprise AI programs. Require every leader to use ChatGPT, Claude, or Gemini for at least one real work task every day for 30 days. This builds intuition faster than any training program and breaks down the 'AI is someone else's job mindset.

For example, in a traditional supply chain, planners estimate demand using past data and heuristic experience. In an AI-first supply chain, predictive algorithms learn from constantly arriving data instead of relying on gut feelings. People plan strategy using machine intelligence instead of hand predictions.

AI-first thinking drives on these assumptions:

- Data- instinct and not gut-instinct guides decisions.
- The processes improve and change constantly.
- Humans + AI create value together.

3.2 Mindset Over Machines

Many companies start their AI journey by investing in models, cloud, platforms, and vendors, hoping technology will change them. People, not clouds, make businesses smart.

AI-first leaders see data, automation, and algorithms as growth tools, not additional work. AI-first culture values learning over knowing, curiosity over comfort, and collaboration over leadership.

3.3 Need for Leadership

Any change begins with leadership, including AI. CxOs of an AI-first company need not be technical, but they should understand intelligence. They should know enough about machine learning to ask the right questions and human behavior to handle automation fear.

AI-savvy leaders always do three things:

- They argue that AI empowers people. By emphasising augmentation, they help teams see AI as a performance partner.
- Evidence guides their decisions. Data-backed insight is essential in meetings, but intuition helps.
- They are optimistic and cautious. AI cannot solve all problems, and smart leaders know when to use their judgment.

3.4 Cultural Transformation

Enterprises must move from AI POC to using it regularly. They should make AI training mandatory to foster curiosity, celebrate early AI wins, and shift incentives to AI outcomes rather than outputs. There should be a organization wide training plan and training calendar with mandatory and optional AI trainings.

AI for leaders training should a completed by every leader. All employees should be enabled with subscriptions like Coursera, Udemy and deeplearning.ai. Enterprises can collaborate with IIMs/IITs/premier institutions to enable executive education on AI and its impact.

Enterprises should make usage of AI tools such as ChatGPT, Claude and Gemini mandatory to be used in day-to-day tasks. Rewards and recognition should be modified to track AI usage.

The C-suite should make clear AI decisions to model leadership.

Tip: Replace 'AI project' language with 'AI capability' language in every internal communication. Projects end; capabilities compound. This framing shift signals to the organization that AI is a permanent part of how you work — not an initiative with a finish line

3.5 Human + AI collaboration

AI-first thinking changes how people and algorithms work together, not machines. Machines can process more data faster, but humans can provide context, empathy, and morality.

Consider AI a smart but literal intern who has a knack for patterns but not nuances. AI benefits from good questions, limits, and values. AI illuminates hidden ideas, helping people think deeper.

Hybrid workflows show this partnership. In finance, AI may find oddities that analysts investigate. Healthcare AI systems may suggest diagnoses, but doctors make the final call. Manufacturing engineers decide when and how to fix AI-predicted problems. Everything is a conversation between human intuition and AI.

Companies that succeed with AI know that coexistence is essential to long-term success.

3.6 Business Processes Transformation

When a company adopts an AI-first mindset, its business processes change in unexpected ways. From the start, intelligence prevails over automation.

Consider a customer service process. Agents wrote down cases manually after customers called. AI-first processes immediately assess how people feel, send the question to the best resource, guess how long it will take to fix the problem, and give the agent real-time coaching. The employee moves from reacting to planning experiences.

AI-first supply chain planning systems can anticipate issues. Sensors feed models real-time data to improve sourcing and logistics. The time between having an idea and acting, called "decision latency," is days to seconds.

Design thinking matters most. Imagine if intelligence were native here. Every process should start with this. That small change makes processes more adaptable and self-learning.

3.7 Ethics and Responsible Intelligence

The story of AI will be defined not only by what we build but by how responsibly we build it. An AI-first mindset therefore embeds ethics as a design principle, not a compliance checkbox.

Enterprise leaders must ask: *Is this model fair? Is it explainable? Who could be harmed if it errors?* Responsible AI frameworks help teams develop systems that respect privacy, avoid discrimination, and remain accountable to human oversight.

Ethical awareness must spread beyond data scientists — HR leaders, marketers, and supply-chain managers all influence how AI outcomes affect people. A culture of responsibility prevents the erosion of trust and ensures that innovation scales sustainably.

3.8 The AI-First Maturity Journey

Growing to be AI-first usually takes five stages:

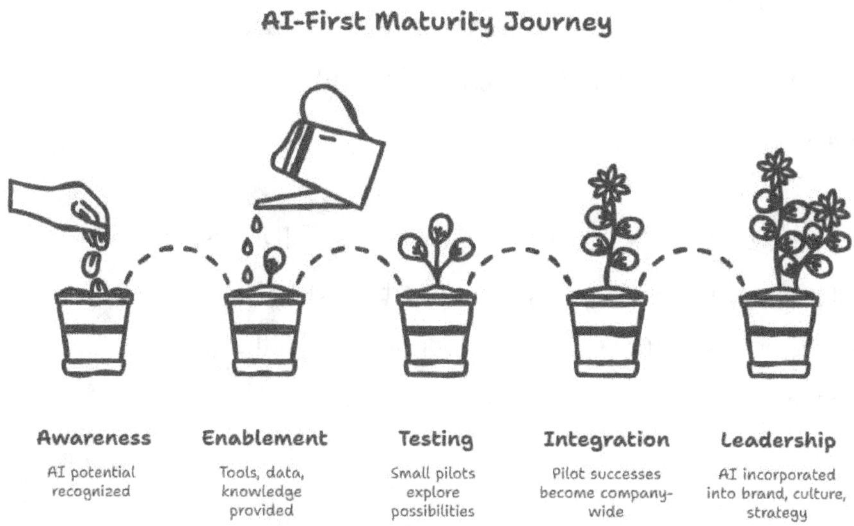

- **Awareness**: The company knows AI has potential but is not sure how.
- **Enablement**: Teams get tools, data, and knowledge.
- **Testing**: Small pilots see if something is possible.
- **Integration**: Pilot successes become company-wide skills.
- **Leadership**: Brand, culture, and strategy incorporate AI.

Each stage requires different leadership. Early on, exploration is most important; later, governance and scale. The final step is self-sustaining intelligence, when the business learns, changes, and grows without technology.

3.9 Conclusion: The Mindset as the Ultimate Differentiator

People are first on the AI-first road. To question years of habits, people should be open to new ways of working together, and see data as more than numbers takes humility. Our thinking will remain constant despite technological advances.

This mindset helps companies lead change as well as respond to it. They will transition from AI projects to smart businesses. Those who see intelligence as culture rather than code will win in the AI age as intelligence becomes the backbone of business.

Chapter 4 –Foundations: Data, Digital, and Design

An enterprise cannot ***win with AI*** until it is AI ready.

AI requires data fluency, digital agility, and careful design to grow. Many businesses build models before foundations. Bad systems, data, and slow processes prevent smart decision-making, which they discover too late.

Businesses can prepare by improving their digital maturity, data DNA, and design principles that link technology to human needs. Imagine making the rail tracks ready before the running of the trains.

The primary components to getting an enterprise AI ready are –

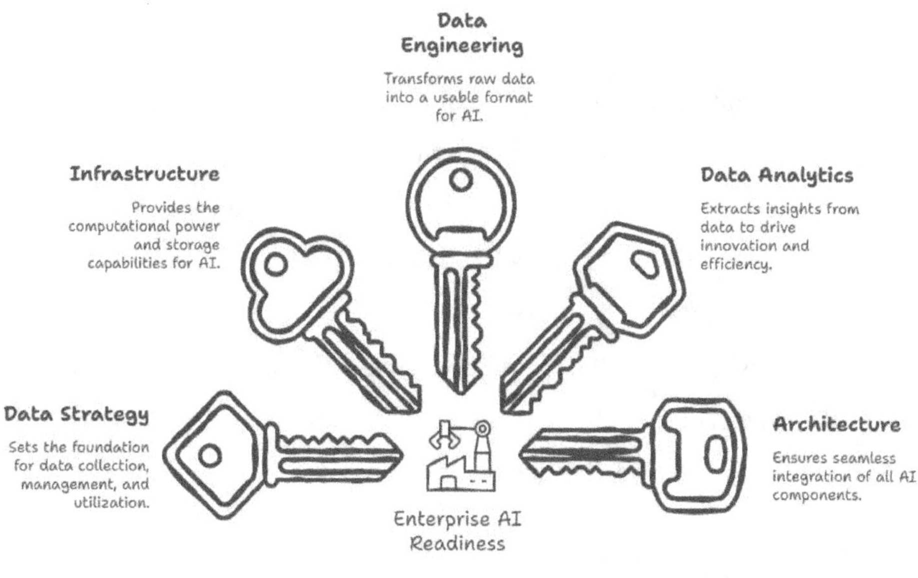

4.1 There Is No AI Strategy Without Data Strategy

Artificial intelligence thrives only where data is abundant, accurate, and accessible.

Yet many enterprises still treat AI ***strategy*** as something separate from their ***data strategy*** — a critical mistake. AI cannot compensate for incomplete or fragmented data foundations. The relationship between the two is not sequential but *symbiotic*: AI goals shape the data systems you build, and your data maturity dictates how far AI can scale.

4.2 Infrastructure

Old infrastructure cannot support AI growth. AI maturity begins with digital readiness.

Cloud computing makes things flexible. It offers flexible data storage, scalable computing, and machine learning platforms. Cloud companies can try new things culturally because development teams can set up environments in minutes instead of months.

Modern businesses prefer composable architectures with modular building blocks instead of monolithic stacks. New features are easy to add when analytics, storage, and visualization are separate.

4.3 Data Engineering and data analytics

Many companies confuse the roles of data engineering, data analytics and AI. This creates confusion over responsibilities. Clear delineation accelerates delivery.

- **Data Engineering**: Builds pipelines for ingestion, transformation, and scalable, high-quality data access.
- **Data Analytics**: Uncovers patterns, insights, and visualizations to inform decisions.
- **AI/ML**: Predicts outcomes and enables autonomous actions beyond mere insights.

They collaborate by the following steps in a race:

1. Data engineers lay the track (clean, accessible data infrastructure).
2. Analysts run the middle leg (turn data into actionable information).
3. AI/ML sprints to the finish (self-improves via learning for predictions/actions).

Retail Example: Data engineers feed transaction/customer data into a warehouse. Analysts spot category trends. AI/ML then personalizes offers per shopper—winning requires all three legs.

4.5 Architecture: Intelligence's Foundation

Even the best AI models fail without robust architecture. Enterprises need integrated data/AI systems spanning infrastructure, tools, governance, and deployment.

Modern Data Stacks contains the following components typically:

- **Sources:** Structured/unstructured data from ERP, CRM, social, IoT.
- **Ingestion:** Streaming platforms, APIs.
- **Storage:** Cloud warehouses, data lakes.
- **Processing:** ETL, feature stores.
- **Consumption**: Dashboards, APIs, AI applications.

An AI strategy should include tasks for creation of reference architectures to be followed by different projects and teams.

4.6 Closing Reflections

Before enterprises aim for AI-first, they must be data-ready, digitally agile, and design-conscious. Digital systems create speed, data creates intelligence, and design creates trust. Together, they form the tripod of AI success.

Winning with AI is not about the sophistication of your models — it's about the maturity of your foundations.

Chapter 5 – Designing an Enterprise AI Strategy

We have come to the core concept of this book. The intent of the book title ***Winning with AI*** is to bring AI to transform enterprises and business. And the primary step of doing this is designing an enterprise AI strategy.

Many organizations have *AI projects* but few have an *AI strategy*. Having a separate innovation lab or a handful of data scientists is not a strategy; it is experimentation. The real challenge is aligning every AI initiative with business vision, operational reality, and measurable outcomes.

We have seen a bit about formulating an AI strategy in our chapter 1. This chapter will enable you to build a complete playbook for success with AI.

The eight pillars for an AI strategy are — Vision and Objectives, Business Value Portfolio, Operating Model, Funding Model, Data and Platforms, Risk and Governance, AI Literacy, and Change Management. They do not operate in sequence. They have to be built as part of the AI strategy or roadmap.

Foundations of AI Strategy

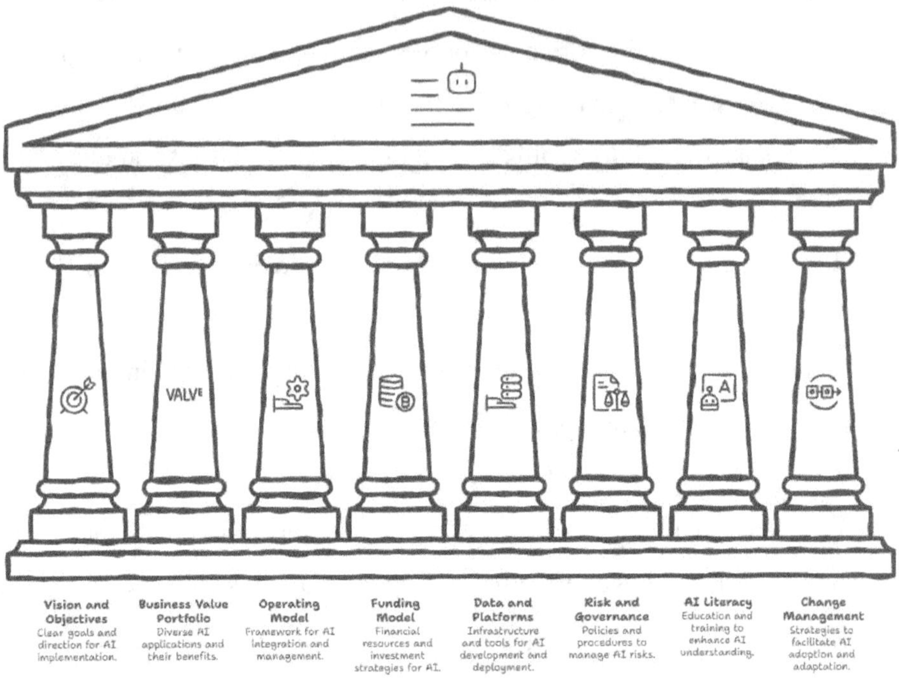

5.1 Vision and Objectives – Our North Star

Every corporate AI strategy starts with the seemingly straightforward question, ***What are we actually trying to become? What essential benefit will AI help create that cannot be created without it, not what equipment to purchase or which procedures to automate?***

This is the vision question, and the quality of the response determines the rest. ***We want to be a data-driven organization*** is an ambiguous response that results in an ambiguous strategy. A clear response, such as ***we will use***

AI to become the lowest-cost, highest-reliability operator in our logistics category within four years results in a plan that can be implemented, evaluated, and monitored.

Vision in AI strategy is not the same as a mission statement. A strategic hypothesis is a precise, verifiable assertion regarding how intelligence will result in a competitive edge in a given market environment. The hypothesis needs to be both specific enough for individuals across the organization to use it as a decision filter and ambitious enough to warrant the investment and organizational disruption required by serious AI transformation.

	Tip: Write your AI vision as a falsifiable hypothesis, not an aspiration. 'We will reduce claims processing time by 40% using AI within 18 months' is testable and fundable. 'We want to be an AI-led insurer' is neither. The discipline of making your vision specific enough to be proven wrong is what separates strategy from wishful thinking.

The goals flow from the vision. Establishing three to five enterprise-level AI goals, each connected to a specific business metric, each with a time horizon, and each owned by a senior leader responsible for delivery, is beneficial for the majority of businesses.

Strategic Theme	AI Objective	Business Metric	Time Horizon
Operational excellence	Optimize supply chain end-to-end	Reduce logistics costs by 25%	3 years
Customer intimacy	Personalize every customer interaction	Lift conversion rate by 20%	18 months
Risk resilience	Detect fraud in real time	Cut fraud losses by 30%	2 years
Sustainability	Minimize energy waste in operations	Reduce energy per unit by 15%	2 years
Revenue growth	AI-driven cross-sell and upsell	Increase revenue per customer by 18%	2 years

These goals serve as the guiding principle for all AI investments and the standard by which all proposed projects are judged. No matter how technically interesting it may be, an initiative that can't be linked to at least one business goal shouldn't be on the roadmap.

5.2 Business Value Portfolio

Once we know where AI can give you a strategic edge, the next step is to decide where to start and how to plan the investments. The business value portfolio sees the AI roadmap as an investment portfolio that is structured, managed, and evaluated based on risk-adjusted return.

Every business has more possible AI uses than it can afford, have the right people, and have the time to work on all of them at once. By looking at use cases from three different angles, you can make a practical and defensible list of priorities.

Business value looks at how the use case will affect the business's strategy and finances if it works. ***Will it change a key metric by a significant amount?*** Feasibility checks to see if the organization has the data, skills, and infrastructure to get the job done in a reasonable amount of time. Adoption potential looks at whether business users will trust and act on the model's results. This is important because a technically great model that no one uses is worth nothing to the business.

Tip: Switch every AI project brief from asking 'What is the model's accuracy?' to 'What business metric will change, by how much, and when?' This single question reframe catches the vast majority of projects that would have been technically successful but commercially irrelevant.

5.2.1 Prioritization

An AI portfolio that is well-made covers three time periods at once, each with a different strategic goal.

Horizon	Focus	Timeline	Examples
Now	Efficiency and automation	0–12 months	Invoice processing, churn prediction, quality inspection
Next	Prediction and optimization	12–24 months	Dynamic pricing, network optimization, personalization
Beyond	Transformation and reinvention	24+ months	Autonomous operations, AI-native products, generative design

5.2.2 POC to POV

Most of the times AI projects fail when they move from testing to production. The reasons are always the same: bad integration with business processes, broken data governance, no clear ownership after the pilot ends, and KPIs that measure how well the model works instead of how it affects the business.

Changing the way you think about every experiment from a Proof of Concept to a Proof of Value changes the design focus from the beginning. From the start, architecture must be ready for production, not added later.

Business users need to be involved in the design process, not just get things at the end. Before development can start, success metrics must be set in business terms. Before any code is written, the migration path must be clearly laid out. This includes who will own the model after the pilot, how adoption will be measured, and what the transition process will look like.

5.3 Operating Model Framework

A great AI strategy and a bad operating model will have the same effect as a great recipe and a bad kitchen: the idea is good, but the execution is bad.

The operating model is the structure, roles, processes, and governance mechanisms that make AI strategy work. It decides whether AI capabilities grow over time or stay broken up forever.

5.3.1 Centralized Vs Decentralized

Every AI operating model has to deal with a basic conflict between centralization and decentralization. The table below shows the pros and cons of three common ways to structure things.

Characteristic	Centralized CoE	Fully Federated	Hub-and-Spoke
How It Works	Single team owns all AI development	Each business unit builds independently	Central CoE sets standards; business units own delivery
Strengths	Consistency, governance, efficiency	Speed, business relevance, domain expertise	Balance of governance and agility
Risks	Slow, disconnected from business, creates bottlenecks	Duplication, inconsistent standards, governance gaps	Requires strong coordination and communication
Best For	Early-stage enterprises building foundations	High-maturity, high-trust organizations	Most enterprise contexts at scale

For a good reason, most mature businesses use the hub-and-spoke model. It keeps the good governance and efficient infrastructure that centralization makes possible while giving business units the freedom to make decisions that lead to useful, adopted solutions.

5.3.2 Center of Excellence for AI

The CoE is the center of knowledge and the backbone of the company's AI operations. It is not a group of data scientists who are cut off from the real world of business; its value comes from how well it connects different parts of the business. It has duties in four areas.

- **Standards and enablement**
- **Platform and infrastructure**

- **Governance and risk**
- **Capability Development**.

Standards and enablement include the best practices, templates, reusable parts, and methodological frameworks that all businesses use to build AI. Platform and infrastructure refers to the shared technology base that business units use to build on instead of duplicating it. Governance and risk includes the processes for reviewing and approving models, bias audits, the model inventory, and following the rules. Capability development includes things like training programs for employees, mentoring business unit teams, and hiring and keeping technical talent.

5.3.3 Governance Architecture

Effective AI governance operates at three distinct levels, each with different stakeholders, cadences, and focus.

Governance Level	Led By	Focus	Cadence
Strategic	Executive AI Steering Committee	Priorities, investment, cross-functional alignment	Quarterly
Operational	AI CoE and Model Risk Team	Model lifecycle, performance monitoring, retraining	Monthly / continuous
Ethical	Ethics Board / Legal / Compliance	Explainability, societal impact, regulatory compliance	Per deployment + periodic review

Level One: Strategic Management

The Executive AI Steering Committee is in charge of this. The top level of the AI governance architecture is strategic governance. It is there to answer the questions that only top management can answer: What kind of AI should this company make and what kind shouldn't it? How much money should be put into what? How do you deal with conflicts between AI priorities in different parts of the business? And who is ultimately responsible when AI has effects, whether they were planned or not, on a large scale?

Level Two: Governance of Operations

The AI CoE and Model Risk Team are in charge of this.

Strategic governance tells you where to go, and operational governance tells you how to get there. Every day, it is important to make sure that AI models are built well, deployed safely, monitored closely, and retired properly when they are no longer useful. Operational governance is where AI risk is either dealt with or where it builds up until it becomes a crisis. The Model Risk Team and the AI Center of Excellence are in charge of operational governance together. The CoE is in charge of technical depth and standards. The Model Risk Team has the independence, regulatory knowledge, and risk assessment methods needed to make a credible challenge. Together, they make up the operational backbone of the governance structure.

Level Three: Ethical and moral Oversight

The Ethics Board, Legal, and Compliance are in charge. The third level of the governance architecture deals with questions that neither strategic governance nor operational governance can answer on their own: ***Is what we're doing right? Not just technically correct or good for business, but really right in terms of how it affects the people and communities that our AI systems touch?***

The governance function that is most often set up last and most often lacks resources is ethical oversight. It is also the function whose absence leads to the most long-lasting and harmful organizational failures. This is because ethical failures in AI usually lead to results that hurt people, hurt the organization's reputation, and are hard to fix once they become public.

5.4 Funding Model

AI transformation needs a different way of thinking about investments than traditional technology programs. Most companies start by funding AI as a series of projects, with separate budgets for each one. These projects are judged on the same timeframes and return expectations as infrastructure upgrades. This method consistently underinvests in the things that determine the long-term value of AI, which leads to the boom-and-bust pattern that many early AI programs follow.

The Compounding Asset Mindset: AI's abilities grow over time in ways that regular tech investments don't. As models get more data, they get better, which means that investing in data infrastructure pays off more and more. When AI developers use shared platforms and reusable components, the cost of each new use case goes down. This makes AI development more cost-effective. And decisions made with AI stop losses and find chances that wouldn't have been seen otherwise.

The Three-Stream Funding System: Mature businesses use three different types of funding that work well together to create both strategic depth and grassroots innovation. Under executive mandate, top-down enterprise investment funds the strategic foundations—data platforms, CoE operations, and governance infrastructure—with multi-year budget commitments that don't change every year. Bottom-up innovation funds work like an internal venture fund. They give small amounts of money quickly to business units to try out new ideas, and they give more money only if the ideas work. Partnership and ecosystem investments give the business access to specialized skills and let it share research and development costs with tech partners, start-ups, and academic institutions.

Characteristic	Project-Based Funding	Compounding Asset Mindset	Three-Stream Funding System
Investment Approach	Separate budgets for each project	Invest in data infrastructure and shared platforms	Top-down, bottom-up, and partnership investments
Timeframe & ROI	Same as infrastructure upgrades	Abilities grow over time	Strategic depth and grassroots innovation
Cost-Effectiveness	Underinvests in long-term value	Cost of new use cases goes down	Access to specialized skills and shared costs
Decision Making	Limited by traditional metrics	AI decisions stop losses and find chances	Strategic foundations and internal venture fund

Tip: Fund AI in three streams simultaneously — top-down strategic investment (platforms and CoE), bottom-up innovation grants (fast experiments at business unit level), and partnership/ecosystem investments — rather than a single monolithic budget. Each stream serves a different innovation horizon and together they prevent the boom-bust cycle that kills most enterprise AI programs

5.5 Data and Platforms

If vision is the heart of an AI strategy, data and platforms are the body.

The level of AI ambition is limited by the quality of the data foundation. The speed and dependability of AI delivery depend on how well the technology architecture fits together. And the governance of both decides if AI can be used responsibly on a large scale.

The Five Stages of Data Maturity

Data is what makes AI different. Models trained on high-quality, proprietary, domain-specific data give you advantages that your competitors can't easily copy. But to get this edge, companies need to treat data like a strategic asset, just like they do with money.

Dimension	Key Question	Failure Mode
Availability	Are sources integrated and accessible?	Real-time decisions on stale data
Quality	Is data accurate, complete, and consistent?	Model failure due to corrupted inputs
Ownership	Are domains assigned to stewards?	No one resolves conflicts; standards drift
Lineage	Can models trace inputs for audit?	Unexplainable behavior; regulatory exposure
Privacy	Is data used with consent and protected?	Regulatory breach; erosion of trust

The Modern AI Platform Stack

You need to choose and design the technology architecture based on rules that will still be true as the landscape changes. The main ideas are modularity over monolith, open over closed, governance-first design, and reuse over rebuild. The stack usually has the following layers.

Platform Layer	Function	Example Technologies
Cloud Infrastructure	Elastic compute, storage, managed services	AWS, Azure, GCP
Data Lakehouse	Unified, governed data storage and access	Databricks, Snowflake, BigQuery
Orchestration	Reliable, automated data pipelines	Apache Airflow, dbt, Prefect
Feature Store	Consistent, versioned, reusable model inputs	Feast, Tecton, Vertex AI Feature Store
MLOps Platform	Experiment tracking, training automation, deployment	MLflow, Kubeflow, SageMaker
Model Registry	Versioning, documentation, lifecycle management	MLflow Registry, Azure ML, W&B
Serving Infrastructure	Low-latency, high-availability model inference	Seldon, BentoML, TorchServe
Monitoring and Observability	Real-time performance, drift, and system health tracking	Evidently, Fiddler, Arize
API Management	Secure, governed model consumption	Kong, Apigee, AWS API Gateway

The AI strategy should assess and provide list of tools to be used by different AI teams. The decision of build vs buy is taken by the AI council in consultation with various stakeholders. The tools list should be validated by security and AI governance teams and the lists should be published on a common forum.

Generative AI: A New Strategic Layer

The emergence of LLMs has introduced a new layer of strategic complexity. For most enterprises, a tiered approach balances capability with cost and control.

Scenario	Recommended Approach	When to Use
General language tasks	Use foundation model via API	No proprietary data advantage
Domain-specific tasks	Fine-tune foundation model on proprietary data	Performance gap justifies investment
Core competitive capability	Build specialized model from proprietary data	Unique data creates durable moat

5.6 Risk and Governance

The risks of AI range from pilot failure with no ROI to harms that affect entire businesses, such as damage to individuals, damage to copyrights, breaking the regulations, damage to reputation, and systemic failures that affect millions.

Risk and governance are the most important pillar of AI strategy. The following are the risk categories we need to address.

Risk Category	Description	Example
Model Risk	Incorrect, biased, or harmful outputs	Discriminatory credit scoring by postcode
Data Risk	Privacy violations, quality issues, breaches	Unconsented personal data usage
Operational Risk	Over-reliance without oversight	No appeal for automated decisions
Reputational Risk	Public backlash from opacity/unfairness	Exposed biased hiring algorithm
Regulatory Risk	Non-compliance with AI laws	EU AI Act breach in high-risk use

Responsible AI is based on the following principles –

- **Fairness**: No systematic disadvantage; validated via technical and impact assessments.
- **Transparency**: AI-influenced decisions meaningfully explainable to stakeholders.
- **Accountability**: Clear model owners for performance and impacts.
- **Privacy**: Consent-based, minimized, protected data use.
- **Robustness**: Reliable under real conditions, including edge cases.
- **Human oversight**: Consequential decisions require effective human review.

Cross-functional AI Governance Board reviews high-impact models pre-deployment and monitors risks. Use model risk classification (by harm potential/reversibility), bias audits, incident response protocols, and regulatory tracking to operationalize principles. Build upfront or face costlier fixes later.

5.7 AI Literacy

People are the most important part of bringing changes to an organization.

Organizations do not change because of technology. **People do**. And people can only change organizations with technology they know how to use well enough to use it effectively, question it in a constructive way, and keep making it better. AI literacy, or the ability of employees at all levels and in all departments to use AI in a meaningful way, is one of the best investments a business can make, but it is also one of the most often overlooked.

A lack of AI literacy leads to a series of organizational problems that quietly hurt even the best AI programs. Business leaders who can't question AI recommendations either trust outputs they don't understand too much or ignore insights they can't judge, both of which ruin the value the model was meant to create. Frontline workers don't like tools that seem unclear or like they could hurt their judgment. Data science teams that don't understand the business build models that don't work. And the company creates a permanent, self-reinforcing gap between the people who make AI and the people who are supposed to benefit from it.

Some tasks for the AI strategy team to improve AI literacy –

- AI fluency certification
- Formation of AI champions team
- Formation of AI CoE
- AI for Leaders
- AI Hackathons
- Rewards and recognition for high ROI AI projects

5.8 Change Management

If an AI strategy treats human change as a secondary concern—something to be dealt with after the models are built and the platforms are up and running—it will fail. The change that AI brings about is really a change in people. The technology is the thing that starts the change; the organization is the thing that is changing. And if you don't pay close attention to how people are dealing with that change, the best technical features will stop being used.

AI change management is different from regular change management in three important ways that require a different approach.

- AI projects are experimental and have probabilistic outcomes
- AI changes may involve more leadership oversight
- AI changes need more governance and control

5.9 Example Spotlight: Unilever's Enterprise AI Roadmap

Unilever's AI journey exemplifies strategic coherence.

The company didn't launch random projects; it built an enterprise roadmap guided by a single vision — to make every decision data-driven and sustainable.

- ***Supply Chain**: AI algorithms forecast demand across 190 countries, reducing waste by 15 %.*
- ***Marketing**: Advanced analytics personalize digital campaigns in real time.*
- ***Sustainability**: AI tracks energy consumption across factories, identifying optimizations.*
- ***Governance**: A global "AI Academy" and ethics council ensure responsible use.*
-

By connecting AI to both profitability and purpose, Unilever transformed intelligence into culture.

***References**:*

https://greyb.com/blog/unilever-ai-food-supply-chain/

https://sloanreview.mit.edu/article/ai-ethics-at-unilever-from-policy-to-process/

https://emvide.com/ai-powered-sustainability-how-unilever-cut-waste-by-40-with-predictive-analytics-2/

https://www.hul.co.in/news/2025/can-factories-run-entirely-on-renewable-energy/

5.9 Closing Thoughts: Strategy as a Living System

An AI strategy is never ***done and dusted***. It evolves with data maturity, business cycles, and emerging technologies. Summary of the AI strategy formation is below :

Pillar	Depends On	Enables
Vision and Objectives	Business strategy, leadership alignment	All other pillars
Business Value Portfolio	Vision, data availability, capability assessment	Funding decisions, CoE roadmap, adoption planning
Operating Model	Portfolio size, governance requirements	Delivery speed, standards quality, scaling capacity
Funding Model	Business value evidence, executive sponsorship	Sustained investment in all other pillars
Data and Platforms	Funding, ownership clarity, governance	Model quality, development speed, reuse
Risk and Governance	Operating model, regulatory context	Responsible deployment, regulatory access, trust
AI Literacy	Learning infrastructure, champion network	Adoption rates, use-case generation, governance quality
Change Management	Leadership commitment, incentive alignment	Everything

The most successful enterprises treat strategy less as a document and more as a *living system* — continuously fed by feedback, refined by learning, and guided by vision.

As you design your enterprise AI strategy, remember:

- Begin with a goal, not a model.
- Make sure your goals are based on real data.
- Scale through rules and structure.
- Make things valuable before they get complicated.

Doing these four things consistently, and AI stops being a toy project, it becomes the nervous system of your enterprise.

\

Chapter 6 – Building the AI Operating Model

Most enterprises run into the same problem: having an AI strategy is not the same as being able to use AI. The **operating model** is the architecture that connects people, processes, platforms, and governance to make AI goals a reality.

AI is not just a bunch of random experiments. Models are made but never go into production. Business units do the same work over and over. Governance only shows up when something goes wrong. At scale, leadership sees dashboards full of pilots and not much value.

Setting up the operating model and the roles, responsibilities form a crucial set of tasks for the AI strategy team.

This chapter builds the organizational engine that makes AI a permanent institution, not just a temporary project.

The AI Operating Model answers the most practical questions in the transformation journey:

- Who decides which AI use cases get funded and prioritized?
- Who evaluates and provides tools for AI for the enterprise?
- Who tracks the AI projects across the enterprise?
- How do central teams collaborate with business divisions without creating bottlenecks?

- Where does accountability sit when a model underperforms or causes harm?
- How does the organization scale what works without losing speed or quality?

This chapter builds the organizational engine that makes AI a sustainable enterprise capability — not a periodic initiative but a **permanent, evolving institution**.

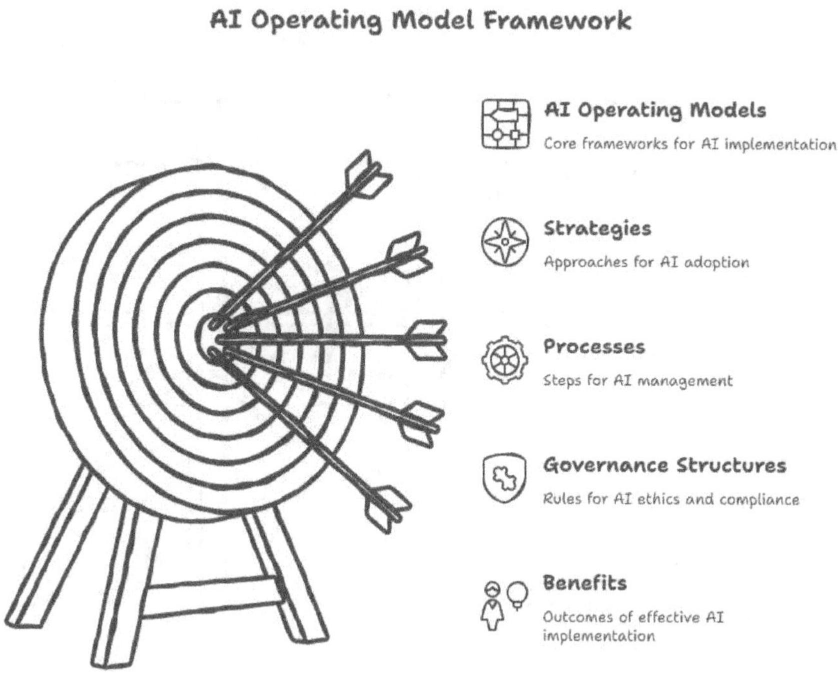

6.1 Restructuring the organization for AI

The traditional enterprise structure—hierarchical, function-based, and matrix—was not designed for AI. AI needs people from different departments to work together, try new things all the time, and have rules that let things move quickly without losing track of who is responsible.

Most businesses set up AI in three different ways. One of the most important decisions an AI leader will have to make is which one to pick.

Centralized vs. De-centralized vs. Federated AI Models

	Centralized	De-centralized	Federated
Team Structure	Single team handles everything	Each business unit has its own team	Center enables, business units execute
Governance	Consistent rules	No required central governance	Governance built into the process
Scalability	Does not scale	Teams build AI that works well	Combines governance with flexibility
Duplication	No duplication	Duplicate work	Sharing infrastructure cuts down on duplication
Data Silos	No data silos	Data silos get bigger	Communities of practice share information
Best For	New businesses, industries with rules	Big companies, early testing	Most big companies long-term

Centralized

The AI Center of Excellence (CoE) is usually the team that does everything. They are in charge of the tools, rules, strategy, and execution. The central team builds and deploys things when business units ask them to.

There are a lot of talented people, rules that are always the same, and technology that works the same way everywhere. The bad news is that it doesn't grow. As demand for AI grows, the central team is becoming a bottleneck. Business units stop owning things and instead build "shadow" capabilities to get around it.

> *A global insurance company built a central AI unit with 60 people. Delivery was good in the first year. By the third year, there were more than 80 requests in the backlog, and business units were quietly making their own analytics tools to get around the queue.*

Best for: new businesses or industries with a lot of rules, like banking, healthcare, and defense, where following the rules is the most important thing.

De-centralized

Each business unit has its own AI team, tools, platforms, and plans for the future. There doesn't have to be any central governance. If there is coordination, it happens in an informal way.

The best part is that teams make AI that works well for them, a lot of people use it, and there is no approval hierarchy that slows things down. The bad thing is that five teams are working on the same model and are doing the same thing twice. Data silos grow. There is no longer any rule. You get a lot of technical debt.

> *A global media group let teams in different parts of the world make their own recommendation engines without help from anyone else. They ran into three different data schemas that didn't work together and no common evaluation criteria when they tried to make a single global platform. In the short term, speed; in the long term, chaos.*

Best for: big companies with very different lines of business or companies that are still in the early stages of testing.

Federated (Most People Should Use This Long-Term)

Most big companies end up with the federated model. It combines the strict rules of centralization with the freedom of decentralization. The center does not have power; it gives people power. This is also known as the **hub-and-spoke** model.

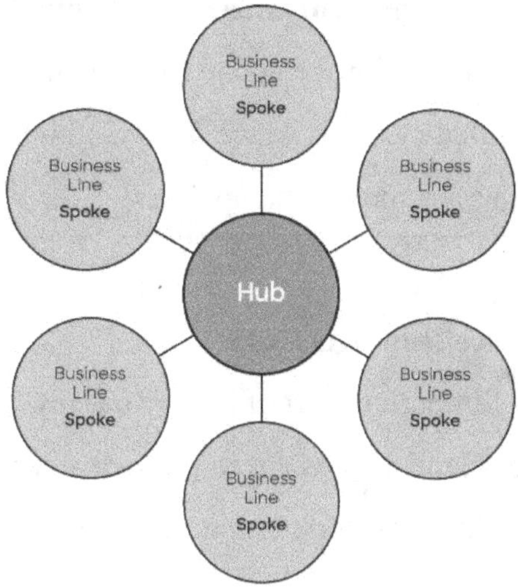

A central CoE (hub) makes rules, shared platforms, and ways to run things. Business units (spokes) are in charge of execution, which means building and deploying AI within those limits. Sharing infrastructure helps to avoid duplication. People in communities of practice share information. Governance is a part of the process, not something that is added on at the end.

> *For instance, a model was used by a global pharmaceutical company in its research and development, supply chain, and sales. The central team kept a shared data infrastructure and an ethics board. Each function had its own AI programs that it ran. The outcome: 40% faster model development and a governance record that passed regulatory audits with flying colors.*

Tip: Start in a **centralized** way to build discipline. As your skills improve, move from central to **federated**. The federated model is where most medium- to large-sized businesses should end up.

6.2 AI Centre of Excellence (AI CoE)

The CoE is the most important part of how you run your business. It is not just a group of data scientists; it is also a group that acts as an architect, coach, gatekeeper, and innovator all at the same time.

A CoE that doesn't have a clear job description goes off course. It turns out to be a cross between an internal consulting firm and a delivery factory, but it doesn't do either job well.

The mandate should include four things:

- **Build**: basic platforms, shared models, and engineering standards.
- **Enable**: Train teams, make toolkits, and speed up adoption.
- **Govern**: Keep the quality of the model, the ethics frameworks, and the readiness for compliance.
- **Be creative**: Try out new AI and use it in a responsible way.

One financial services CoE started without a clear purpose and quickly got overwhelmed with random requests. After a reset, leadership changed its role from "deliverer" to "enabler." Because business units now had the tools to do things on their own, project delivery across the company tripled in just one year.

You will have a lab if you only hire data scientists. You will only get slide decks if you hire strategists. To work together, you need to be good at both business and technology.

In a mature CoE, the most important people are the **Chief AI Officer** (or Head of AI Strategy), who is comfortable in both boardrooms and engineering reviews; the **AI Architects,** who design the enterprise platform; the **Senior Data Scientists and ML Engineers**, who lead model work and mentor others; the **MLOps and DataOps Engineers**, who keep everything running in production (often undervalued, but always critical); the **Business Translators**, who connect strategy and science; the **AI Ethics and Risk Officers**, who build governance in from the start; and the **Learning & Development Leads**, who run AI fluency programs across the organization.

A small business needs between 5 and 10 people to be the right size. A medium-sized group of 15 to 40 people. A global company might need 50 to 100 people at the center, and even more people working in business units.

The most common reason why CoE fails is that it becomes a new bottleneck with a fancier name, which is exactly what it was meant to stop.

Some ways to avoid failing the CoE:

- Give everyone access to shared artifacts like models, code libraries, and governance templates so they can use them on their own.
- Create internal AI incubators, which are short, structured programs that help business teams move quickly with the help of the CoE.
- Set up Communities of Practice, which are monthly meetings where professionals talk about issues and how to fix them.
- Move CoE talent to different business units to speed up adoption and bring domain knowledge back to the center.
- Create levels of control. Not every model needs a full review by the CoE. Make sure that the level of oversight is right for the risk.

> *A logistics company set up its governance in levels. Low-risk models only got a light review, medium-risk models had to go through a structured impact assessment, and high-risk models had to go through full CoE and ethics board scrutiny. The time it took to review low-risk cases went from six weeks to four days.*

6.3 New roles and teams

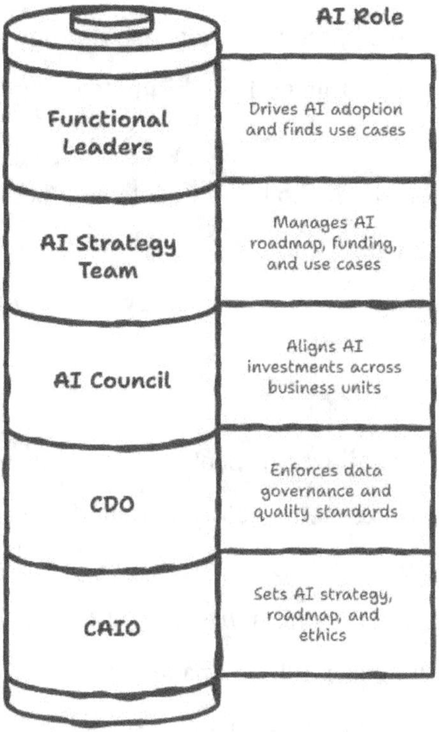

Chief Data Officer (CDO)

The CDO is in charge of the company's most important AI resource. Their job is to create and enforce the data governance framework, make data catalogs and quality standards, set up access policies, make sure the data strategy is in line with AI goals, and teach everyone in the company how to use data.

Chief AI Officer (CAIO)

The CAIO is the newest and possibly most important person in the C-suite. They are in charge of the AI strategy, roadmap, and portfolio; lead the CoE and federated AI program; set the organization's ethics policy and risk tolerance; keep the board up to date on AI progress; and create the organization's AI talent strategy from hiring to culture.

A great CAIO is someone who knows a lot about both business and technology, is okay with not knowing what will happen, is a good communicator, and can see how technology will change society in the long term.

The new CAIO of a retail group spent the first 90 days listening to and visiting different business units before writing down any plans for the future. She figured out that trust, not technology, was the biggest problem. Business managers didn't think it was possible to make sense of AI outputs. The first thing she did was make a framework for all of the models that customers could see that explained how they worked. You need to build the base before you can reach your goal.

Functional Leaders

Functional leaders in supply chain, finance, HR, and marketing are the ones who know the most about how AI can help. Because of this, they are the most important people for getting people to use it. They find use cases that will have a big effect, give out resources, encourage people to use them, share their domain knowledge with data science teams, and make sure their employees act on AI-generated insights.

> *A VP of the supply chain said that all planning meetings had to start with a review of AI forecasts before anyone could change them. That one change in policy changed the culture from "AI as a suggestion" to "AI as the starting point." The rate of overrides dropped from 45% to 18%, and the accuracy of forecasts got a lot better in just two quarters.*

AI Strategy Team: Making the Vision Happen

The **AI Strategy Team** is a small group of senior staff who work closely with the CAIO. Their only job is to make sure that the enterprise AI roadmap is clear, has enough money, and stays on track. The CoE takes orders from the AI Strategy Team. It doesn't make models; it changes the conditions that make it possible for the right models to be made.

Core responsibilities include owning the enterprise AI use case portfolio, which means deciding which projects to start, which to keep going, and which to end based on their strategic value and feasibility; managing the AI investment thesis and business case development for major programs; keeping an eye on AI market trends and finding relevant opportunities before competitors do; and turning board-level priorities into CoE and business unit roadmaps.

An AI Strategy Team that works well is like an internal pressure test. They ask tough questions about whether a proposed AI project will really help the business, whether the data is there to support it, and whether the company can handle it. AI portfolios often get full of pet projects and proof-of-concepts that don't really do anything if they don't have this feature.

A global logistics company discovered that its AI portfolio had grown to more than 60 active projects, but there was no clear way to prioritize them. The AI Strategy Team's first job was to look over the portfolio and get rid of 30 projects, combine 15 more, and make room for the 10 most valuable programs to move faster. In just two quarters, the value of AI investments had doubled. This wasn't because they added more resources, but because they stopped spreading them so thin.

AI Council: Aligning Across Businesses

The AI Strategy Team is in charge of the plan, and the AI Council is in charge of making sure that everything is going according to plan. The CAIO usually leads this cross-functional governing body, which includes senior representatives from each major business unit, the CIO, CDO, Chief Risk Officer, and legal. Its job is to make sure that the company's AI investments make sense, that different business units aren't working against each other, and that all of the company's top leaders agree on how AI is doing and what risks it poses.

The Council meets once a month or every three months, depending on how well the organization's AI is doing. It checks the AI portfolio against strategic goals, decides how to use resources when priorities conflict, approves big new investments, and gives executives a look at governance and risk. It also talks about cultural and adoption barriers that leaders may not have heard about before. These are the problems that slowly kill AI programs without anyone noticing. You need to know the difference between the Ethics Review Board and the AI Council.

The Ethics Board makes sure that models are safe and follow the rules, while the Council makes decisions about strategy and investments. In real life, they work together. The Council decides what is most important and how much money is available, and the Ethics Board makes sure that those priorities are followed.

6.4 Ethics and Risk

You cannot just check off AI governance before you go live. From figuring out what the problem is to retiring the model, it's a constant discipline that runs through every stage of the AI lifecycle. There are many examples in the history of AI that show how dangerous it can be: hiring algorithms that were biased against women, credit models that were biased against minorities, and facial recognition tools that got people's names wrong. In most cases, ethics was just a formality. The results—regulatory exposure, legal implications, lost trust, and real harm to people.

Inquire about the individuals impacted by this decision and assess if any group may face disadvantages. Before you touch any data, do a bias risk assessment. Write down what you plan to do with it and make it clear what is not in scope.

Below are some steps for ethics and risk assessment.

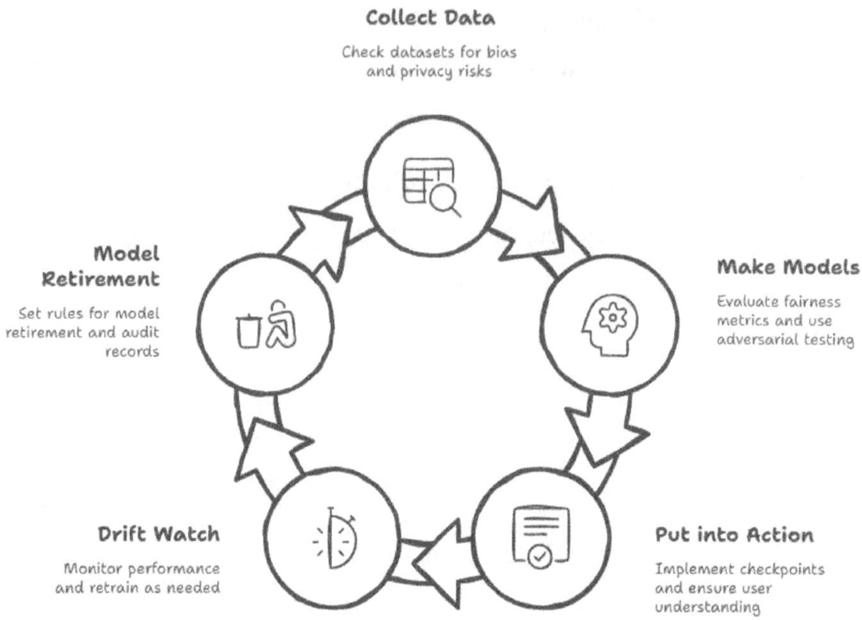

Collecting Data

Look for historical bias, gaps in representation, and privacy risks in datasets. Stick to the rules for keeping data to a minimum. Keep full records of the lineage, such as where the data came from, who approved it, and when it was last checked for accuracy.

Making Models

Check out fairness metrics that are more than just accuracy, such as precision parity, demographic parity, and equalized odds. Use tools that will help you figure out what the model has learned. Use adversarial testing to find bias and things that could go wrong.

Putting into action

For important decisions, make sure that everyone is aware of the checkpoints. Make sure the people who will be using the model understand what it says and why it says it. Make sure the people who will read the document know what it can't do.

Drift watch

Keep an eye on performance all the time to see if it gets worse, drifts, or stays the same. Set up alerts to go off automatically when something strange happens. As the business changes, make sure to set up regular ethics reviews and retraining.

Model Retirement

Make sure there are clear rules for when a model should be put to bed. Throw away anything that is old, dangerous, or no longer useful. Keep track of things for the audit.

Every sprint at a health tech company included an ethics review. Before the readmission risk model was put into use, the review found that it was less accurate for older patients. The imbalance was fixed by a targeted data augmentation program, and the final model worked just as well for people of all ages.

Your AI Risk List

Every business should have a living AI risk register that lists: data risk (bad, biased, or non-compliant data); model risk (overfitting, drift, or unintended generalization); operational risk (pipeline failures, version conflicts); compliance risk (GDPR, CCPA, or sector regulations); reputational risk (AI decisions that hurt groups or damage trust); and strategic risk (investments that don't give value).

Assign someone to be in charge of the risks in each category. Check every three months or after the model changes a lot. Send big problems to the AI Governance Board.

6.5 The Board of Ethics

A formal AI Ethics Review Board makes big companies more responsible to the public. The CAIO, the chief risk officer, an independent outside ethics advisor, business unit representatives, and a customer advocate are all members of the CAIO.

The board approves the use of high-risk systems, looks into ethical violations, sets and updates the AI ethics policy, and compares its work to changing global standards.

The Ethics Review Board of a financial services company stopped using an automated loan approval model when they learned that zip code data was unintentionally acting as a proxy for race. Four months later, the model was changed and passed the review. This delay kept the company from having to deal with possible regulatory action and a big hit to its reputation.

6.6 Final Thoughts

The more clearly you define structure, the more freely innovation flows. This is a paradox at the heart of building an AI Operating Model.

When teams know who owns what, what rules apply, and how governance works, they stop waiting for permission and start making things. When shared infrastructure gets rid of technical problems, ideas get to production faster. When ethics are built in from the start, trust grows, and trust leads to adoption.

Every operating model, regardless of industry or scale, succeeds or fails on five things:

- **Clear Strategic Mandate**. AI's role is explicitly defined, communicated, and linked to business outcomes. No ambiguity about why it matters or what it's expected to deliver.
- **Accountable Governance**. Every AI initiative has a named owner, a defined risk profile, and a governance path proportionate to its impact. Accountability is human — not diffused across teams.
- **Shared, Scalable Infrastructure.** Data platforms, model registries, and MLOps tooling are reusable across the enterprise. Teams build on common ground.
- **Embedded Ethics and Risk Management**. Governance is a design discipline, not a deployment checkpoint. Ethics officers, fairness audits, and explainability standards belong in every project lifecycle.

- **A Culture of Continuous Learning.** Teams learn from every model — success or failure. Knowledge flows through communities of practice, internal showcases, and shared documentation.

The AI Operating Model is not a bureaucracy; it is the operating system that runs enterprise intelligence. If you plan it out carefully, the organization you build will be smarter, more flexible, and more ethical than any one model or project could ever be.

Companies that win with AI don't just use the best models. They make the smartest companies.

Chapter 7 –Technology & Architecture Blueprint

Buying a platform, hiring some data scientists, and then waiting for results, is like using AI without architectural coherence. This cannot be part of any AI strategy. We need a technology backbone to have the AI working.

Infrastructure, data, model operations, and security are the four foundations that decide if enterprise AI works reliably, scales responsibly, and provides lasting value. Each one changes the others.

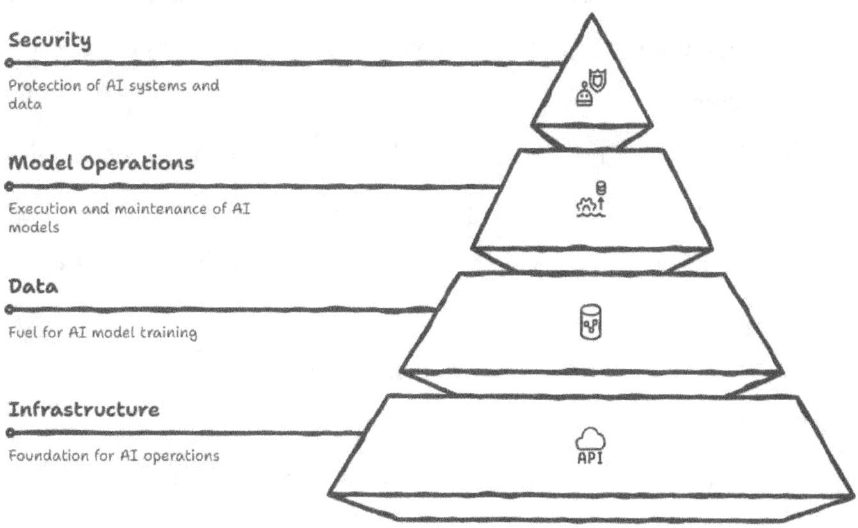

7.1 Infrastructure

Every business must first answer the question, "***Where does the intelligence really live?***" before they can build anything.

The answer is more complicated than most people think.

AI algorithms, data, applications using AI, business intelligence and everything to enable AI.

The Five-Layer Stack

There are five layers that make up enterprise AI, and each one has its own job.

- The **Data Foundation** collects and stores raw data from all sources, including transactions, sensors, CRM platforms, and document repositories.
- The **Data Processing** layer above it takes that raw data and cleans it up, adds to it, and organizes it so that models can use it.
- Data scientists use the **Model Development Environment** to try out new things, train, and test them.
- The **Deployment and Operations** layer takes models from the lab and puts them into use.
- And the **Application** Layer is where AI finally meets the user, through dashboards, APIs, alerts, and other tools.

The Edge, Multi-Cloud, and the Cloud

Without the cloud, no modern AI architecture can grow. You can store more data, scale up and down, and use AI services that would be too expensive to set up on your own with cloud platforms.

AWS has the most services, Azure works well with Microsoft business environments, and Google Cloud is best for TPU infrastructure and modeling data that is already in the cloud. More hyper scalars are available offering many services including GPU rentals.

Most big businesses use more than one cloud not because they want to, but to avoid being stuck with one, meet data residency requirements, and save money.

Smart technology is built into devices like factory sensors, retail terminals, and medical monitors thanks to edge AI. This lets them decide right away without having to go online. When you need to make a choice quickly, when the connection is not stable, or when you can't legally send raw data off the device, the edge is the best place to do it.

> *A semiconductor company put AI models directly on sensors on the production line. Models found defects in real time and sent out alerts right away, with no cloud latency. The rate of defect escape fell by 40%.*

7.2 Data: The Base That Everything Else Stands On

The modern data stack is the set of tools that lets smart apps get AI-ready data from source systems. Most businesses should put more time and money into it.

From Data Warehouses to Lakehouses

Traditional data warehouses were made for reporting, with structured data, batch loading, and SQL optimization. AI needs something more dynamic than what analytics warehouses were made for, like different types of data, real-time ingestion, and access patterns.

Three different architectures have come about as a result of evolution.

- **Data warehouses** like Snowflake and BigQuery are still the best tools for structured historical analysis.
- **Data lakes**, like AWS S3 and Azure Data Lake, hold a lot of raw data in any format. Platforms like Databricks Delta Lake were the first to create the lakehouse. It combines the flexibility of a lake with the governance and query performance of a warehouse.
- The **Lakehouse** is the default architecture for AI in most businesses today because it lets you do both analytics and machine learning with one governed data asset.

> *A store moved from a regular warehouse to a Databricks lakehouse. Twenty-three different data sources came together on one controlled platform. Six months later, AI teams could see real-time transactions, historical trends, and unstructured customer reviews all in the same place. This made models that weren't possible before.*

Nowadays, most of the data platforms have embedded AI enabled so that they can provide AI services on the same server where the enterprise data exists.

Feature Stores

People often don't think about two parts of the modern data stack until they are gone and it hurts. Engineered features are kept in **feature stores** so that models can use them.

Without one, different teams will make slightly different versions of the same input on their own. This will lead to models that aren't consistent, work that is not useful, and results that can't be compared. With one, features are the same in both training and production.

They are shared, versioned, and documented. The last point is more important than it sounds: training-serving skew, which happens when a model behaves differently in production than it did in testing because the data transformations weren't the same, is one of the most common and annoying reasons why models fail.

Vector databases

Vector databases are the second thing that people don't give enough credit to, and now that generative AI is becoming more popular, they are needed. Large language models store information in high-dimensional vectors, which are numbers that stand for meaning.

Vector databases keep these representations and let you search through them on a large scale. This makes semantic search possible, which understands intent instead of just keywords. It also powers retrieval-augmented generation (RAG) apps that connect LLMs to business knowledge.

> *A company that offers professional services made an AI assistant that is linked to 50,000 documents. The keyword search came back with noise. The assistant used a vector database and RAG to answer questions like "What are our standard contractual terms for EU data processing agreements?" by finding the right clause in the right document with great accuracy.*

Streaming: Realtime responses

AI models that get batch data can only talk about things that have already happened. Models that get data from streaming sources can react to what's going on right now.

Apache Kafka and AWS Kinesis capture data flows in real time, Apache Flink and Spark Streaming change data as it moves, and platforms like Tecton compute and serve features in milliseconds. For things like fraud detection, real-time personalization, or live operational optimization, streaming infrastructure is a must. It's what makes a system do something instead of just reporting.

> *A ride-sharing platform went from batch demand forecasting (updated every four hours) to streaming (every 60 seconds). The new system responded to real-time demand patterns during surge events and made drivers 28% more available during peak hours.*

7.3 Model operations(MLOps)

MLOps solves the hardest part of AI: not building models, but keeping them alive in production. It turns the model lifecycle — data prep, training, validation, deployment, monitoring, and retraining — from a manual craft into an automated, repeatable pipeline.

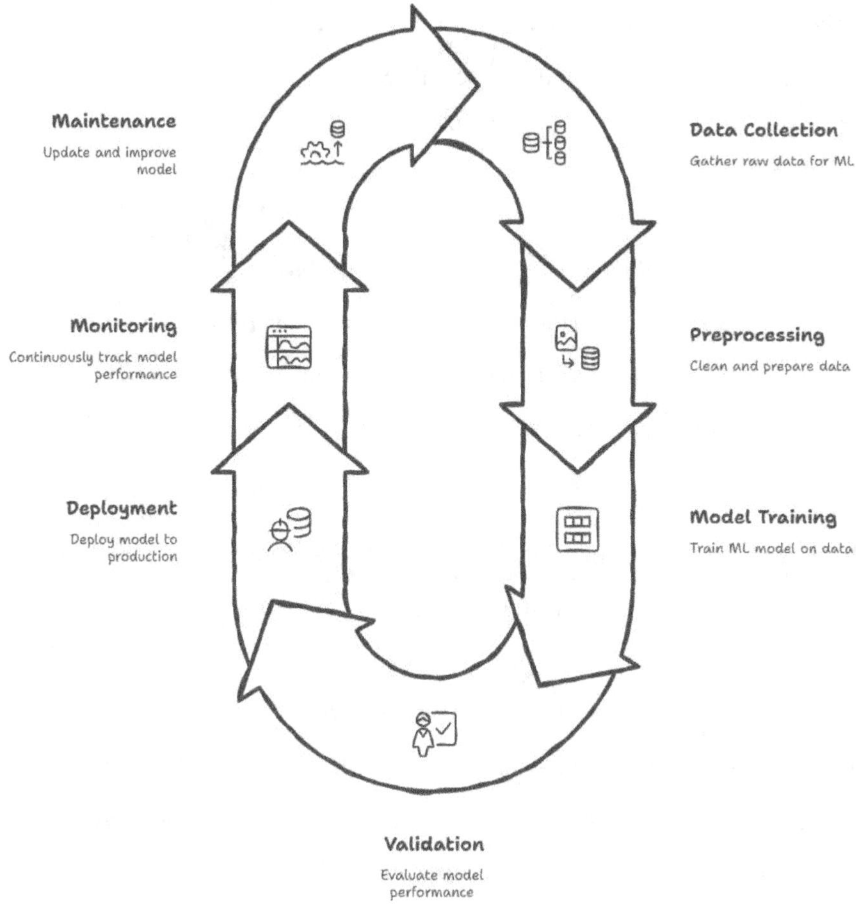

Key practices mirror software engineering: experiment tracking (MLflow, W&B) makes runs reproducible; CI/CD pipelines test and deploy new versions automatically; model registries track what's live in production; and monitoring tools catch drift and degradation before they become problems.

Without it, every step is disconnected and done by hand. With it, the whole lifecycle is controlled and scalable.

> *A worldwide insurance company set up an MLOps platform on AWS SageMaker. The time it took to deploy a model went from 6–8 weeks to 4 days. More importantly, there were no more incidents of model degradation, which is when bad models stayed in production without anyone noticing.*

Model drift is where the model behavior and accuracy deteriorates with new data coming into the system. It happens slowly and without any noise.

Data drift happens when real-world inputs don't match training data anymore, like when markets change or people act differently. Concept drift is even worse: the connection between inputs and outputs breaks down completely. *For example, a credit risk model that worked well before a recession stops working during one.*

The way to control this is keeping an eye on dashboards that have statistical thresholds, automatic retraining triggers, and regular reviews of their assumptions.

Some of the things that traditional AI models do are classifying, predicting, and making recommendations. Generative AI models can read and write language for a lot of different things. That generality is both good and bad. A linked LLM can answer questions, write documents, look at reports, and make code. If it doesn't have the right architecture, it can also make things up, leak private information, or give outputs that are against the law.

RAG: Putting enterprise data into LLM context

The most common way to connect LLMs to business knowledge is through Retrieval-Augmented Generation. RAG doesn't use a model's pre-trained knowledge, which might not be up to date or complete. Instead, it gets relevant documents from business sources at the time of inference and adds them as context. The answers are based on information that is up-to-date and specific to the company. There are a lot fewer hallucinations. You don't have to retrain the model to change what you know. And source attribution lets users check answers, which is very important for businesses.

Fine-Tuning and Agents

Fine-tuning changes a base LLM to fit the needs of a business when RAG is not enough. This is because the model has to always use the same tone, follow reasoning that is specific to the domain, or use language that is specific to the domain. LoRA, or Parameter-Efficient Fine-Tuning, has made this possible by training small adapter layers while keeping the weights of the base model the same.

Things get interesting when AI becomes agentic. LLMs don't just answer questions anymore; they also do things like breaking down complicated tasks, calling APIs, writing and running code, starting workflows, and bringing in other specialized agents when they need to.

Finance, procurement, and customer service are already using it in the real world. But if AI has this much freedom, governance can't be an afterthought. You need to limit what agents can do on their own, get human approval for anything important, and keep a full record of everything they do.

> *A company hired a procurement agent to keep an eye on commodity prices, look over supplier contracts, and point out chances to renegotiate. It cut the time analysts spent on research by 65% and found $12 million in ways to improve contracts in its first quarter.*

7.4 Security, compliance, and technology

AI systems that manage sensitive data and make critical choices are highly desirable targets. Security and compliance must be incorporated into every design decision from the start; they cannot be added later.

The rules are simple to comprehend, but adhering to them requires discipline. Get only what you truly require. Data collected for one purpose cannot be used for another without authorization. Limit access to training sets, model outputs, and raw data to specific individuals and objects. Data should be anonymized as much as possible before entering training pipelines.

AI methods that protect privacy give businesses that need to advance real choices. Federated Learning does not store all of the raw data in one location; instead, it uses data from multiple sources to train models. Every node builds its own model and only exchanges model updates. Differential privacy makes it statistically impossible to deduce the meaning of each record by adding random noise to the data. Synthetic Data Generation creates fictitious datasets that are statistically identical to authentic ones. This allows you to maintain the training patterns you require without disclosing actual personal information.

> *Federated learning was used by a healthcare network to teach a diagnostic AI model across 12 hospitals without any patient records leaving those hospitals. The model worked just as well as one trained on centralized data, but it followed all privacy rules.*
>
> *A logistics company went through almost the same steps: in Phase 1, they used demand forecasting; in Phase 2, they used real-time route optimization; and in Phase 3, they used an LLM-powered operations assistant. Each step added to the one before it. The work on data quality in Phase 1 made the models in Phase 2 more accurate. The structured operations data from Phase 2 made the*

> *Phase 3 assistant much more useful than a generic deployment would have been.*

Main threats on models are:

- **Adversarial inputs** are data that has been changed in a way that makes the model behave differently.
- **Model inversion** is the process of figuring out how to get training data from outputs.
- **Prompt injection** is when bad inputs are used to change how a system works (this is a unique weakness of generative AI).

Defenses include adversarial robustness testing, output filtering, differential privacy during training, and regular red-team exercises that focus on AI.

Rules to follow for compliance by region

- GDPR says that automated decisions must be explainable and that data collection should be kept to a minimum.
- The EU AI Act says that high-risk AI (like hiring, credit, and healthcare) needs to be open, have human oversight, and be tested for bias.
- The CCPA controls how consumer data is used in California. Sector rules add more requirements on top of these.

7.5 Closing Reflection: Architecture as Competitive Advantage

Architecture is not a technical issue; it is a strategic one. The choices made today about data storage, model deployment, generative AI integration, and governance will affect how competitive the next ten years will be.

The company with the most AI projects is not the smartest one. It is the one with the best AI infrastructure, which is a machine that turns data into decisions and decisions into results.

In the end, architecture is about how a business decides to think.

Chapter 8 – People and AI Fluency

People make the most important asset for any enterprise.

When everyone in a company knows how to use AI, it becomes even more important for the business. The more leaders want everyone to know how to use AI, the more likely it is that they will be able to.

Companies that spend a lot of money on platforms and models but don't pay attention to the people who use them always do worse than companies that build technology and people skills at the same time. The main difference between an AI strategy that works and one that doesn't is whether or not the company got its people on board.

AI transformation is not something that people use. They are the most important part of its infrastructure.

People always come back to the same point when they talk about AI: an algorithm that is the most advanced in the world is useless if the people around it don't understand it, trust it, or use it.

Companies that spend a lot of money on platforms and models but don't pay enough attention to the people who use them always do worse than those that build technology and people skills together. The difference between an AI strategy that stays on slides and one that makes a difference

is almost always this: did the company get its people on board?
AI transformation doesn't use people. They are its main infrastructure.

In this chapter we will cover the new roles for AI transformation and the AI training required.

8.1 The Roles AI Transformation Actually Needs

AI strategy emphasizes creating some new roles in the organization so that they inculcate the importance of AI and focus on implementing the strategic initiatives.

Few roles are below:

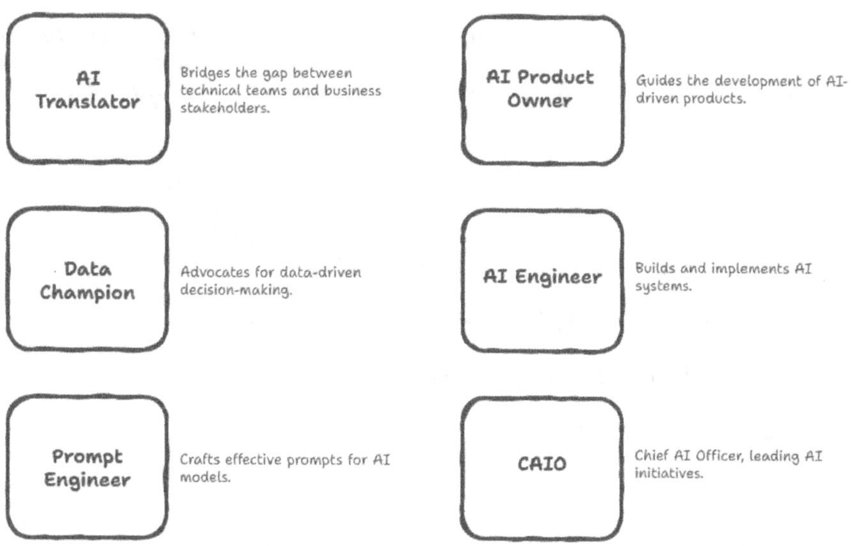

The **Chief AI Officer (CAIO)** is in charge of the company's AI strategy, makes sure that investments are in line with business goals, manages risk, and makes sure that AI projects grow beyond small pilots into full-fledged organizational capabilities.

AI Translator is the most important job that people forget about. It sits between business and data science, turning messy business problems into clear AI questions and turning model outputs into recommendations that executives can use. Sets realistic expectations for what AI can and can't do. Usually comes from within—experienced analysts or operations managers who have a good sense of data.

> *For six months, a planning manager didn't use a demand forecasting model. Then, they changed the outputs to "confidence bands," and adoption went from 20% to 85% without changing the model.*

AI Product Owner : Makes sure that models provide business value, not just technical beauty. Defines problems, keeps track of the model backlog, measures performance against business goals, and chooses when to retrain, redesign, or retire.

> *Within a year, all five of a telecom's strategic models got better. This wasn't because the data scientists got better; it was because someone now owned the bridge between science and strategy.*

Data Champion - This person is in charge of data quality, governance, and literacy at the domain level and works with other business functions. Allows the central data team to work with more people without having to hire more people.

Emerging Roles - As AI gets better, new skills are becoming available, such as Prompt Engineers, AI Ethics Analysts, MLOps Engineers, and Human-AI Interaction Designers. Not everything is needed on the first day, but planning for them early stops the talent gaps that can quietly ruin programs.

8.2. Building AI Fluency at Scale

The most common mistake people make when they try to improve their AI skills is to think of it as a technical problem. The idea is that if you train the data scientists, the rest of the company will follow. In reality, it's almost the opposite. Technical talent is important, but there aren't many of them, and they mostly work on their own. The bigger chance and the bigger problem is getting the thousands of non-technical employees who will decide whether or not AI insights are acted on to be fluent in AI.

8.3 What an Enterprise AI Learning Program Looks Like

Upskilling is not a one time effort. It is ongoing. With AI growing exponentially every month, the employees need to stay up-to-date.

To start with, the components that matter most for AI learning are

- AI Foundations course accessible to everyone
- Functional bootcamps tailored to specific domains
    - AI for Supply Chain
    - AI for Finance
    - AI for HR
    - AI for IT
    - AI for Trainers
- A data literacy curriculum covering interpretation, visualization, and critical evaluation
- Leadership seminars covering AI governance and transformation strategy
- Certification pathways that recognize and reward capability development.
- Specialized trainings on LLM prompt engineering, fine tuning, RAG, Agents and automation.
- Trainings on Coursera, Udemy, Deeplearning.ai and IIT, IIM, Great Learning and ISB executive education courses.

The focus on practical work is very important. Learning that includes working with real business data is much better than learning abstract theory. One of the best ways to speed things up is to have managers take part. When leaders train with their teams, adoption rates go up a lot.

> *DBS Bank made foundational AI education mandatory for all 33,000 employees, with role-specific pathways and a separate*

> *leadership module covering governance and strategy. Within two years, employee-driven AI innovation ideas increased fivefold, and the bank's AI deployment pipeline accelerated significantly — much of it attributed to improved business-user capability and confidence.*

8.4 Low-Code Platforms as Democratization Tools

One of the best ways to make AI more accessible is to simplify its use. Power BI with Copilot, Snowflake, Tableau, DataRobot, Alteryx, and Salesforce Einstein allow business users to create analytical models and automate workflows without writing code, turning AI users into active contributors.

Power without rules is dangerous, so governance is crucial. Citizen data scientists can create inaccurate, immoral, or unchecked models. The AI CoE provides pre-approved data sources, templates with best practices, and a way to review any decision-generating model.

> *A logistics company equipped its operations planning team with Alteryx and pre-approved datasets. Within three months, planners were building their own route optimization analyses. Fourteen models were created — all CoE-validated before going live. Planning cycle time dropped 30%, and the central data science team's backlog cleared by 40%.*

8.5 Automation Anxiety Is Real

Fearing AI will eliminate jobs is reasonable. Historically, people have lost jobs to automation. AI rarely eliminates jobs; it make jobs better and easier. Repetitive, rule-based, or data-heavy tasks are most vulnerable. Judgment, empathy, creativity, and relationship management are harder to automate. New jobs usually require different skills than lost ones.

Ignoring automation anxiety only makes it harder to spot. Employees secretly fight AI tools, work around them, and harm projects. The other option is to be open about which processes are changing and why, be honest about role changes instead of brushing off concerns, give real examples of coworkers who have successfully made the switch, and—most importantly—get employees involved in redesigning AI-supported workflows.

> *An insurer implementing AI-driven claims processing that would automate 60% of routine assessments ran a six-month "Future of Work" program before deployment. Claims assessors attended workshops exploring what their role would look like post-automation and were retrained for complex claims requiring empathy, negotiation, and regulatory judgment. Adoption was near-universal. Attrition during the transition was negligible — and assessors subsequently reported higher job satisfaction because the repetitive triage work they'd found draining was now handled automatically.*

8.6 Building Trust in AI Outputs

Workers who aren't worried about losing their jobs may distrust AI outputs for good reason. Models can screw up. At first, recommendations may seem odd. Being skeptical when an algorithm contradicts an expert is not a cultural failure; it's reasonable.

Sharing a model's conceptual, not technical, workings builds trust because users know what signals it responds to. After years of accurate advice, skeptics believe. Accepting that you don't know everything makes models that show confidence levels more reliable than those that show all outputs with the same confidence. Being clear about what led to a recommendation helps users think about it instead of just accepting or rejecting it.

> *A consumer bank's credit team resisted an AI model replacing their manual scoring framework. The CoE ran "model explanation workshops" showing how the model weighted key factors — and, crucially, compared its predictions against officer intuitions on historical cases, including cases where the model had been wrong. The transparency built credibility. Within six months, officers were using the model as their primary tool and flagging divergences — creating a feedback loop that improved the model further.*

8.7 Change Management

AI changes cannot be managed with a single communication campaign. It operates on three levels.

- We must increase awareness, skills, and honest conversations about what's changing and why at the individual level.
- The team level requires changing workflows to accommodate AI tools before they are used, setting adoption goals with visible recognition, and empowering early adopters to be change agents.
- Organizational leaders should use and discuss AI insights, plan and evaluate processes that use AI outputs, and update HR policies to reflect that AI is making work easier.

The order is crucial here.

8.8 Incentives and Collaboration Models

Motivation makes people act. Assuming AI adoption but not rewarding it will always compete with project delivery, quarterly numbers, and headcount management. See, value, and recognize AI contributions like other strategic contributions to get real adoption.

Some periodic rewards can be AI tool credits, books on AI, shout outs, monetary rewards and other gifts.

> *One MNC ensured that every leader who completed a set of AI courses was given 5% increment.*

8.9 Making AI Fluency a Career Accelerator

An organization's strongest message is that AI skills help people advance in their careers. These include making AI literacy a core competency in performance reviews, recognizing employees who identify or promote AI use cases, providing clear career paths from data champion to AI translator to AI product manager, and prominently featuring AI contributors in internal communications.

> *A manufacturer added "AI Contribution" as a formal dimension in its performance review process — equal in weight to safety, quality, and operational excellence. Within two performance cycles, employee-initiated AI proposals increased 300%. The signal was unambiguous: contributing to AI transformation was core to professional growth, not optional.*

8.10 Innovation Incentives

Targeted innovation incentives accelerate grassroots adoption and career advancement. Teams of employees compete in timed internal AI hackathons to solve real business problems and generate new ideas while improving their skills. Employees can test new ideas without capital approval with an AI Innovation Fund. Recognition programs and internal showcases honor successful deployments and their creators, leading to more AI contributions.

8.11 Cross-Functional Teams and Communities of Practice

- **Multidisciplinary squads** - the highest-value AI work happens at the intersection of domains. Effective teams combine a data scientist, data engineer, business domain expert, AI product owner, UX/process designer, and ethics/compliance reviewer. Harder to assemble, but eliminates the rework cycle of technically strong models that nobody adopts.

- **Communities of Practice (CoPs)** — peer-driven networks that share challenges, accelerate knowledge transfer, reduce duplication, and surface hidden talent across geographies.
- **Making CoPs work requires four things:** dedicated time for members, a persistent home base, public recognition of contributors, and letting the community set its own agenda rather than using it as a top-down broadcast channel.

> *A pharma company's AI community of practice grew from 12 founding members to over 400 participants across 30 countries in two years. Monthly sessions featured internal case studies, external speakers, and open problem-solving. Innovations deployed in one region reached other regions in weeks rather than the months required by formal knowledge-transfer programs.*

8.12 Measuring Where You Are - Workforce AI Maturity Model

A maturity model gives enterprises a structured way to assess their current state of workforce AI fluency, identify priority gaps, and plan targeted interventions. Unlike technology maturity models, this one is entirely people-focused. The Five Stages of this are :

AI Adoption Stages

Stage	Description
1 — Unaware	AI is IT's domain
2 — Emerging	Awareness is growing
3 — Developing	Structured learning paths exist
4 — Proficient	AI fluency is embedded
5 — Intelligent Organization	AI fluency is expected

The maturity model is best for diagnosing and planning, not ranking. Start by assessing the situation, such as employee surveys, training participation, and AI adoption data. Map by function—business units will be at different stages. Stage 3 of the supply chain and Stage 1 of HR may occur simultaneously.

Set 12-month goals for each function to advance one level, not the entire organization to Stage 5. Set target interventions based on function status. Repeat every six months.

A global consumer goods company mapped all 15 business units against the five stages. Manufacturing and supply chain were at Stage 3; marketing at Stage 2; HR and legal at Stage 1. Rather than running one universal program, the company designed tailored interventions for each stage. After 18 months, every function had advanced at least one stage, and the average enterprise AI adoption rate had climbed from 38% to 67%.

Chapter 9 – Responsible, Ethical and Sustainable AI

It's easy to treat ethics as a checkbox when using AI to stay competitive. Just add it at the end, give it to legal, and move on. It's a mistake and getting more expensive. Companies that start with responsibility in their AI strategy don't just avoid trouble. They create systems that last, gain trust quickly, and improve decisions. This chapter covers how to do AI without regret.

9.1 Ethics, Bias and fairness

Unethical AI hurts business. After discovering that an AI recruiting tool always rated women's resumes lower, Amazon is famous for eliminating it. A large U.S. health insurance company was sued because its AI denied claims more often than humans. These were big companies that didn't ask the right questions in time, not small ones trying to save money.

Asking ***Who does this AI affect?*** is easy. ***Could some groups be disadvantaged? What happens if it's wrong?*** Identifying them is easy; asking them during design rather than after the product is out is difficult.

This has two effects on your business.

Choose a leader first. Call them a **Chief AI Ethics Officer**, an AI Governance Lead, or whatever fits your org — just make sure there's a human accountable for asking the hard questions.

Second, **incorporate ethical reviews** into AI development like security reviews. Regular audits, not one-time checks. Do this before anything else.

Not all AI bias is intentional, but it is still a problem.

Models learn from historical data, and history is not always fair. A bank that trains a loan model on ten years of data inherits ten years of discriminatory lending practices. No malice required. The harm scales automatically anyway.

Think of it as a smart student raised on a bad curriculum. The student is not broken, the inputs were.

A few practices to help here -

Go beyond accuracy. A model that's 92% accurate overall but only 74% accurate for a specific demographic isn't a 92% model for those people. Break down performance by gender, age, income, location — whatever's relevant to your use case.

Create model cards. A short document covering what the model does, what data it was trained on, and where it struggles. If your team can't answer those questions, that's the first problem to fix.

Build a feedback loop. Testing never catches everything. Make it genuinely easy for users and employees to flag bad decisions, then actually follow up on those reports.

Accountability. When AI denies someone credit, raises a medical flag, or filters a job candidate, "the algorithm decided" is not an acceptable answer legally or ethically. A real person needs to be able to explain it, and change it.

9.2 Transparency and Trust

People shouldn't trust AI. They read the news. They think it's choosing for them but don't know how. Regain that distrust.

The solution isn't to drown customers in technical details no one reads. Clarify what your AI does, what data it uses, and what rights people have.

A simple example from financial services: some firms now include a single line on customer-facing decisions — something like ***"This recommendation was generated with AI and reviewed by a human advisor.*** " This sets expectations, signals oversight, and tells the customer there's a real person in the loop. That's all it takes to shift the dynamic.

Internally, the same standard applies. Your front-line staff shouldn't be enforcing AI decisions they don't understand or feel they can't question — that's where trust breaks down fastest. Train your people on what the systems do and why, not just how to operate them. Understanding the reasoning matters.

Then there's generative AI specifically. If customers are talking to a chatbot powered by a large language model, they deserve to know it. Most regulators agree — the EU AI Act already requires it, and similar rules are spreading. This isn't a future concern. Get ahead of it now rather than retrofitting compliance later.

9.3 Sustainable AI

Training a single large model can consume as much energy as powering a town per year. At scale, that's a real ESG, regulatory, and talent concern.

- GPT-3's 175 billion parameter model used roughly 1,287 MWh to train. This is about 100 times the annual energy use of the average US household.
- Inference now accounts for 80–90% of all AI computing power training is a one-time cost; inference runs forever.
- Google estimates a median Gemini text prompt uses 0.24 watt-hours of energy and emits 0.03 grams of CO_2

For the long-term sustenance of using AI, we as an enterprise need to adopt the following during architecture.

- **Right-size models** — a fine-tuned smaller model often outperforms a general-purpose large one for specific tasks, at a fraction of the compute cost. Don't reach for GPT-4-class infrastructure by default.
- **Measure your carbon footprint** — tools like CodeCarbon and cloud dashboards track energy consumption per training run. What gets measured gets managed.

- **Build for longevity** — schedule retraining, build monitoring pipelines, and plan for deprecation. An unmaintained AI system is a liability waiting to surface.
- **Pace your organization** — initiatives that burn out teams, skip documentation, or outrun governance will collapse. Build a foundation for the next decade, not just the next quarter.

We don't have to solve climate change. All we have to do is make smarter architectural choices.

Chapter 10 – Measuring Success

Boardrooms are discussing how the company has invested in AI for two or three years. Data scientists can prove their models are accurate. Pilots found interesting results.

When the CFO asks, ***What is this investment really worth to us?***

The room goes quiet.

Technology isn't to blame. Measurement is the issue. Most companies are using frameworks for regular tech projects to evaluate AI. These frameworks have a clear scope, timeline, and measurable results. Not how AI works. It learns. Adds up. Things improve in scattered, connected ways that are often only apparent afterward. Businesses always undervalue it because they don't know how to measure it, which leads to underinvestment and limited change.

This chapter provides frameworks for measuring and managing AI value so businesses can see it, discuss it honestly, and manage it on purpose with boards, investors, employees, and themselves.

10.1 AI Value Creation

AI creates value in three ways, each requiring a different measurement method.

Cost optimization is easiest; it automates tasks, reduces waste, and lowers error costs. The measurement logic is simple: baseline cost minus actual cost minus AI cost. Finding out who did what is hard. It takes discipline to determine the AI's role when many things are changing at once, which often requires running a control group.

Revenue Enablement has the most financial potential. AI outperforms humans in targeting, pricing, and customer retention. A recommendation, price, competition, and time can all lead to a purchase, but the chain is longer. Experimenting AI decisions versus a control group is the most accurate way to measure.

> *One financial services company found that AI-personalized offers had a 23% uptake rate, while standard campaigns had 14%.*

Innovation Creation is the most crucial strategy but hardest to measure. This creates new value streams, not improves them. Real-time underwriting opens new markets. New drug discovery takes eight years, down from twelve. To measure this, you need visible short-term financial results and option value, a careful guess at what new competitive positions AI enables.

10.2 Value Metrics Hierarchy

Mixed metrics at four distinct levels make most measurement frameworks fail.

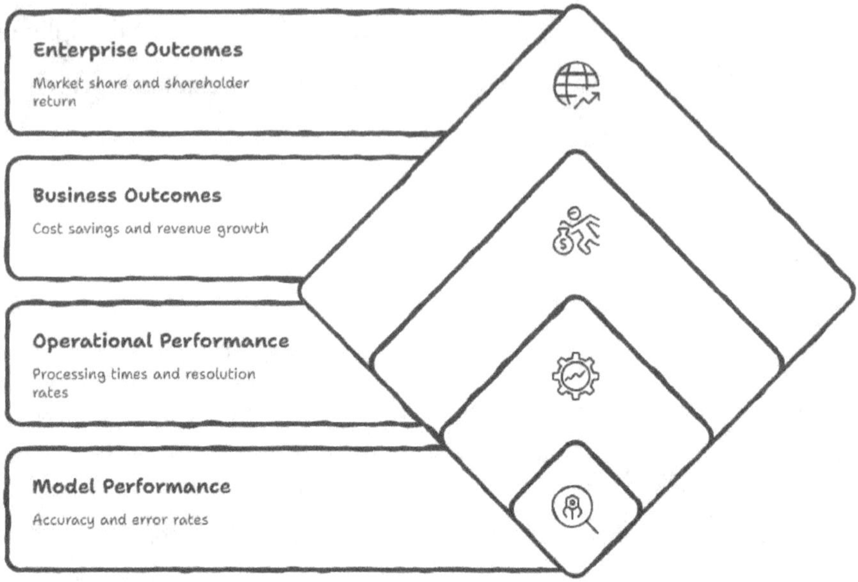

Level 1 - Model Performance (accuracy, AUC-ROC, error rates) tells technical teams if a model works. It's meaningless without context. A 99.2% accurate fraud model sounds good, but doing nothing gets you 99.5% of the time if fraud is 0.5%.

Level 2—Operational Performance links model outputs to business impact like processing times, resolution rates, and downtime hours. Without following its advice or fixing the process, even a very accurate model won't change much.

Level 3—Business Outcomes shows the CFO how AI cuts costs, boosts revenues, and boosts margins. Work with finance to create models using their rules. The framework is more credible when the CFO's team builds the model instead of looking at yours.

Level 4—Enterprise Outcomes—market share, growth rate, and shareholder return—are the best reasons to invest in AI but hardest to separate.

Use three methods: track long-term trends before and after big deployments, compare your results to other companies with different AI profiles, and evaluate all project business outcomes. No single method yields a clean number. When combined, they make something useful for board meetings.

10.3 Economic Impact Models: Beyond ROI

AI investments can grow over time, but standard ROI only considers short-term returns. Four models provide more detail.

The strongest foundation is **decision quality**. Multiply the number of business decisions by their volume, value, and AI improvement to determine how much AI will help.

> *A commercial bank that makes 40,000 small business loan decisions a year, with an average loan amount of $180,000,*

> *thought AI would lower the loan default rate from 4.2% to 2.8%, saving $100.8 million annually.*

The math is easy; doing it is hard.

ROI often misses **time compression value**.

> *A pharmaceutical company reduced the time it takes to find new drugs from twelve to eight, saving money on research and development and generating billions in revenue four years earlier. That speedup may have the highest NPV of the investment. On a smaller scale, a two-week faster financial close gives management two more weeks of accurate data per month.*

Network Effects undervalue AI systems that improve over time. A marketplace matching engine with 500 buyers in its first year seems small. With 5,000 buyers in year three, matching quality improved because the network grew, not the algorithm. To model this, you must guess how fast it will grow, not just its current performance.

Competitive Optionality is the value of AI's strategic options, like entering new markets or precisely defending against competitors, before you use them. Put numbers on them with scenario modeling. The exercise improves strategic vision, regardless of the numbers.

10.4 Better Measures: ROA, Learning Speed

Traditional ROI views AI as infrastructure, which depreciates over time. A well-designed AI system adds up. A customer lifetime value model with a 180% 3-year ROI could reach 800% over ten years. Looking at it over three years undervalues it and discourages investment.

Return on AI Assets (ROA) fixes portfolios. Numerator: the value of all business AI systems. Full capability stack cost, including infrastructure, talent, data platforms, governance, and change management. ROA makes you consider your portfolio, reveals underutilized skills, and rises as the compounding flywheel turns. That trend line is crucial information for an executive team.

Learning Velocity measures AI systems' improvement rate, not just their current capabilities. If one company improves 15% annually in AI and the other stops, they will have very different competitive futures. Monitor model, use-case, and enterprise speed. A velocity drop indicates a learning infrastructure failure before it affects business results. Because it learned slower, a media company discovered that its data quality was declining months before subscriber retention numbers showed it.

10.5 AI as a growing asset

Moving from projects to assets is the biggest AI management change. There are project deadlines. Without further investment, AI in operations depreciates. Competitors, data, and the world change. Assuming AI is done is like hiring a world-class athlete without training funds.

Every model in production has a value, growth path, risk of losing value, and maintenance, according to **asset management**. Expect retraining, improving, and expanding costs in addition to deployment.

> *A large bank gave each AI system a business executive to manage profits and losses and a budget for new ideas. This year's performance and long-term improvement were used to rate owners.*

Automated performance checks and problem identification, cause identification, change implementation, and testing before use are the four steps of the **optimization loop**. Not just a goal, this is a clear strategy. **AI Business Review** makes measurement governance. Monthly operations reviews reveal model and use issues. Quarterly enterprise reviews by the Chief AI Officer, CFO, and COO assess portfolio value and prioritize investments. *An annual review of the company's competitive position and risk. All reviews answer five questions: Portfolio earnings: what? System improvement? In use? Creating what? Why is it important?*

Not keeping an AI dashboard no one reads is best. Add AI metrics to enterprise scorecards. AI adoption on the HR scorecard is HR leaders' responsibility. Operating cost reports credit plant managers for AI savings.

Investors treat AI pipeline value like M&A, giving it the same attention as other strategic commitments.

When new use cases cost less to deploy, deployment speed increases, and portfolio ROA rises, **compounding pays off**. When that happens, the measurement framework no longer reports. It builds organizational conviction and supports AI's long-term investment.

Chapter 11 – AI Governance

AI governance exists to answer three simple questions:

- What AI do we have, and where is it being used?
- What risks does it create, and who is accountable for managing them?
- How do we ensure it delivers business value without violating our security, privacy, or regulatory obligations?

These questions are harder to answer than they appear. In most large enterprises, AI doesn't arrive through a single coordinated program — it proliferates. An HR team deploys a policy chatbot. Finance embeds a summarization tool in its reporting workflow. Developers adopt code-assistance software. Operations experiments with automated ticket routing. Each is a reasonable local decision. Collectively, they create a landscape that is difficult to see, difficult to secure, and difficult to audit.

Governance provides the coherence that prevents this fragmentation from becoming a serious liability. It gives the organization visibility into what it's actually running, a consistent way to assess and manage risk, and shared standards that let individual teams move quickly without each independently reinventing security and compliance practices from scratch.

11.1 The AI Inventory

- You cannot control what you don't measure.

- You cannot govern what you can't see.

Most firms believe they know their AI system count. The majority are wrong. In addition to the big ones, dozens of smaller integrations are happening quietly across business units, including scripts that call model APIs, AI features hidden in third-party software, and tools teams use without telling anyone.

An effective inventory includes the owner, purpose, models and providers, data sources, users affected, and risk classification for each system. To build it, application owners must report on their work and automated discovery must scan cloud environments, API logs, and inventory entries before new deployments go live.

This isn't form. Prioritizing risks, reporting to regulators, and responding to incidents depend on it. Without it, regulators, auditors, and even your leadership can't know what AI you're using.

> *An EU AI Act compliance check revealed 47 active AI systems at a global financial services company. Officially, 19 registered. An API log analysis and voluntary disclosure revealed the other 28, including several that processed customer data. Regulatory review began without knowing more than half of their AI footprint.*

11.2 Governance structure and accountability

Governance goes beyond tech controls. You need a clear organizational structure with roles, decision-making rights, and someone responsible for every business AI decision.

AI Council members come from strategy, IT, security, legal, privacy, and key business units. Government shouldn't slow things down by approving every AI project. It sets rules, allocates resources, resolves standards disputes, and monitors the organization's AI posture. Think hub-and-spoke system center.

The **AI Enablement Team** powers it. They manage the technical platform, including APIs, reference architectures, deployment templates, and advice. They focus on making AI safer than circumventing guardrails. When resourced and responsive, business units are less likely to use ungoverned workarounds.

An **intake process** is a good way to govern. Teams submit a simple use case, data, affected parties, and expected value before starting work. This starts a risk classification that determines scrutiny. More review goes to high-risk projects. Safer ones move faster. Without this, governance follows problems.

> *For AI projects requiring central resources, one large store started with a two-page intake form with six questions. In six months, voluntary submissions tripled, and the governance team had a reliable pipeline view for the first time.*

11.3 Technical Governance

Architecture matters for governance. Governance is nearly impossible to enforce after each team chooses its own models, connects them to any data, and deploys without central control.

Most people choose the **Centralized API Layer**. Use a central API layer to access a few approved AI services, usually hosted in a company-controlled private cloud tenant. Teams create apps on a public platform. More visible governance gives teams more freedom. The wrapper simplifies access control, logging, and usage monitoring.

Data architecture and permissions matter more than most teams realize. AI systems should respect data permissions, but this requires careful engineering. Not just indexing documents in retrieval-augmented generation. The query-time filter must restrict retrieval to what the user requested.

> *A professional services firm learned this the hard way. Early tests with an internal knowledge assistant showed that junior staff could ask the right questions to get private partner pay and client engagement terms. Indexed without permission filtering. This took three weeks to fix. It would have taken three days with permission architecture from the start.*

The rest depends on private cloud hosting, role-based access, and data residency. Healthcare, financial services, and public sector organizations must have these by law. Knowing where data goes in a model prompt is essential for compliance. Not answering that question indicates a governance gap.

11.4 Risk Management

Deploying AI without adequate testing is a governance failure. Because AI outputs are probabilistic, context-sensitive, and can fail, testing it is harder than testing regular software.

At minimum, verify that the system outputs useful data for typical use cases and can handle the expected load with acceptable latency. The bare minimum, and many teams only do that.

Mature governance goes further. Any sensitive data program should use adversarial testing, which involves using prompt injection or social engineering to break the system. Hallucination testing checks if the system fabricates data. Content safety evaluation checks for tricks to produce harmful or illegal outputs.

> *One large bank red-team tested its internal AI assistant for prompt injection before going live. Found twelve flaws. Engineering fixed eight issues quickly, and four required architecture changes.*

> *Adding two weeks to the schedule prevented a major data breach.*

In production, monitor usage, errors, performance, and cost, as well as prompts and responses for traceability, unusual prompting patterns, and model changes. No action is required when model providers update or deprecate versions or change system behavior. You must catch that.

Compliance with regulations changes frequently. Data must be explainable and minimal under GDPR. The EU AI Act restricts high-risk hiring, credit, and healthcare apps. CCPA governs consumer data rights. Sector-specific rules add more layers. The governance team turns these into internal controls and updates them. Treating compliance as a one-time mapping exercise traps organizations when rules change.

11.5 Agentic AI Governance

Everything we've discussed applies to AI systems that create actionable information. Another type of AI is agentic, which does things instead of providing information.

An **agent** may search data sources, run queries, update records, send messages, or call other services. It may store data between sessions. These skills are impressive. They pose risks that regular chatbots don't. An agent that approves something wrong, sends a notification to the wrong person, or changes data without meaning to can cause real harm that can't be fixed by looking at what it said.

Agent design principles must be clear. Specify which tools and APIs the agent can call, under what conditions, and what requires human confirmation before proceeding. Follow the minimal footprint rule: agents should only request permissions they need and prioritize undoable actions. Human-in-the-loop checkpoints are required for data changes and external communications.

> *A manufacturing company tested a procurement agent who could search supplier databases, write purchase orders, and submit them for approval. Uncertain instructions caused a loop of creating and sending duplicate orders when confirmation responses were late during testing. Controlled capture. Possible production impact: hundreds of thousands of dollars in duplicate orders. Clear confirmation before submission and strict retry limits are the solutions.*

Agent governance is a new study. Most companies are developing design patterns. To avoid starting from scratch with governance for the next agent deployment, write down what you learn about design patterns, permission frameworks, testing requirements, etc. if you deploy early.

11.6 Long-term Lifecycle Management

Governance goes beyond project approval. From design to retirement, it must work. Consider it an ongoing discipline, not a gate.

Version and change management involves tracking production model and prompt versions. Before accepting a model update, you must run regression tests. A model change can affect text tone, accuracy, and length in ways that aren't obvious but affect user satisfaction and compliance. One healthcare technology company discovered this after its LLM provider quietly updated the model. Clinicians noted longer responses that sometimes violated protocols. The company used version-pinning to track model changes, find the exact update, roll back within hours, and set regression testing requirements before accepting more updates. Consistent log keeping paid off.

Decommissioning is crucial but often overlooked. Governance must keep and delete logs, clean vector stores and caches, keep audit records, and talk to users after retiring a system. Retired systems running elsewhere can cause compliance issues, security risks, and operations confusion. Non-decommissioning organizations quietly accumulate governance debt. Start ruling now. People don't understand the risks of AI's rapid adoption. Building habits early on gives you organizational muscle as systems become more powerful and important to your work, even if they're not perfect.

Small first step: establish a cross-functional governance body, structured intake process, centralized technical platform, and start taking stock. Starting there, everything else can grow.

Global consumer goods company starts AI governance two years before EU AI Act. The regulation took effect with a full inventory, a working risk classification process, written controls, and a two-year-old governance team. Postponed remediation cost competitors 18 months. The early investment paid for compliance and gave the company the confidence to use AI quickly while others stopped.

Chapter 12 – Summary

To consolidate whatever we have covered so far, I have listed the main points in bullets. This chapter summarizes the creation and maintenance of an AI strategy in an enterprise.

8 Pillars of AI Strategy

- Vision and Objectives
- Business Value Portfolio
- Operating Model
- Funding Model
- Data and Platforms
- Risk and Governance
- AI Literacy
- Change Management

Vision & Objectives

- Start with "*What are we trying to become?*" — not "*What tools should we buy?*"
- Vision must be a precise, verifiable strategic hypothesis, not a vague mission statement
- Establish 3–5 enterprise-level AI goals, each tied to a specific business metric, a time horizon, and a named senior owner
- Any initiative that can't be linked to at least one business goal shouldn't be on the roadmap

Business Value Portfolio

- Evaluate use cases on 3 dimensions: business value, feasibility, and adoption potential
- A technically great model that no one uses delivers zero business value
- Balance the portfolio across 3 time horizons: near-term wins, mid-term bets, longer-horizon investments (~60/30/10)
- Shift from POC (Proof of Concept) to POV (Proof of Value) — production-readiness must be designed in from day one
- Business users must be involved in design, not just handed the output at the end
- Success metrics must be defined in business terms before development starts
- Post-pilot ownership and transition plans must be defined before any code is written

Operating Model

- A great strategy with a bad operating model = great recipe, bad kitchen
- Three structural models: Centralized, Decentralized, Federated
- Centralized: strong governance but becomes a bottleneck at scale
- Decentralized: fast adoption but creates data silos, duplicate work, and governance gaps
- Federated (hub-and-spoke): the recommended long-term model — center enables, business units execute

- The CoE connects strategy to business reality; its value comes from cross-functional bridging

CoE Responsibilities

- Standards and Enablement: best practices, templates, reusable components
- Platform and Infrastructure: shared tech base for all business units to build on
- Governance and Risk: model review, bias audits, model inventory, compliance
- Capability Development: training, mentoring, hiring, retention

Governance Architecture — 3 Levels

- **Level 1 (Strategic):** Executive AI Steering Committee — sets direction, allocates funding, resolves cross-BU conflicts
- **Level 2 (Operational):** AI CoE + Model Risk Team — ensures models are built well, deployed safely, monitored, retired properly
- **Level 3 (Ethics):** Ethics Board, Legal, Compliance — answers "*Is what we're doing right?*" beyond just correct or profitable

Funding Model

- Funding AI as isolated projects with short-horizon ROI expectations consistently underinvests in long-term value
- Treat AI as a compounding asset: as models get more data, they improve; shared platforms reduce per-use-case costs over time

- Three-stream funding: top-down enterprise investment (platforms, CoE, governance), bottom-up innovation funds (venture-style, small amounts, scale only what works), partnership/ecosystem investments

Data and Platforms

- If vision is the heart of AI strategy, data and platforms are the body
- Level of AI ambition is directly limited by data foundation quality
- Design principles for the platform stack: modularity over monolith, open over closed, governance-first, reuse over rebuild
- The AI council (with security and governance teams) should validate and publish an approved tools list
- Generative AI requires a tiered approach balancing capability, cost, and control

Risk and Governance

- Risks range from pilot failure to regulatory breach, reputational damage, and harm to individuals
- Responsible AI principles: Fairness, Transparency, Accountability, Privacy, Robustness, Human Oversight
- AI risk register should cover: data risk, model risk, operational risk, compliance risk, reputational risk, strategic risk
- A Cross-functional AI Governance Board should review high-impact models pre-deployment
- Build governance upfront — retrofitting is far costlier

AI Literacy

- Organizations change because of people, not technology
- Low AI literacy causes over-trust, under-use, or misuse of model outputs
- Key initiatives: AI fluency certification, AI champions team, AI CoE, AI for Leaders program, hackathons, rewards for high-ROI AI projects

Change Management

- If human change is treated as secondary, the strategy will fail
- AI change management differs from regular IT change in 3 ways: outcomes are probabilistic, more leadership oversight is required, more governance and control is needed

Chapter 13 – Industry best practices and tips

Vision & Strategy

- Start with business problems, not technology — work backwards from a specific outcome ("reduce churn by 15%") to the AI approach, not the reverse
- Build a balanced portfolio: ~60% near-term wins, ~30% mid-term bets, ~10% longer-horizon investments
- Secure genuine C-suite commitment — budget protection, decision authority, and visible behavioral endorsement — before launching
- Define explicit success criteria (both technical and business metrics) before any development begins; include a minimum viable impact threshold

Data Foundations

- Conduct a data readiness assessment before committing to any use case; establish quality SLAs for all production data feeds
- Invest in data governance and a data catalog before the AI portfolio scales — lineage, ownership, and definitions must be documented early
- Build a centralized feature store earlier than feels necessary to prevent inconsistent features and training-serving skew
- Leverage synthetic data to unlock use cases blocked by data scarcity or privacy constraints

Operating Model & Governance

- Federate deliberately: define what the center builds vs. enables, publish a clear RACI, and ensure shared infrastructure genuinely reduces duplication
- Tier governance by risk — lightweight processes for low-risk models, full board review for high-stakes decisions (credit, hiring, medical)
- Embed ethics at problem definition, not as an end-stage review; conduct a bias risk assessment before touching data
- Maintain a model registry from the start — recording ownership, performance, retraining history, governance approvals, and review schedules

Talent & Culture

- Hire for curiosity and communication alongside technical skill; test both explicitly in interviews
- Invest in AI translators (business-to-technical bridge roles) — often higher ROI than additional data scientists
- Build broad AI fluency across the organization, not just depth in specialists; measure through behavior change, not training completions
- Create explicit career ladders for AI roles; run annual AI talent reviews to proactively manage retention risk

Execution & Delivery

- Choose first use cases for high feasibility, meaningful value, and visibility — early credibility is a strategic asset
- Run disciplined pilots with defined go/no-go criteria and sunset clauses; kill failures fast and accelerate what works
- Build MLOps infrastructure (CI/CD, model registry, monitoring, automated retraining) before you need it — retrofitting is far costlier
- Report on business impact (churn reduction, cost savings, revenue lift), not model performance metrics like AUC

Generative AI

- Start with augmentation (drafting, summarizing, code assistance) before autonomous deployment in high-stakes contexts
- Default to RAG architecture before fine-tuning — faster, cheaper, updatable, and reduces hallucination; fine-tune only when context injection consistently fails
- Treat prompt engineering as an organizational capability: build a versioned prompt library and test prompts adversarial before production
- Govern for hallucination (treat LLM outputs as drafts requiring human review) and data exposure (classify what can enter model context before deployment)

Common Mistakes to Avoid

- Piloting without a defined path to production ownership and scale

- Beginning model development before data quality and governance issues are resolved
- Treating AI as an IT project — business ownership of use cases and adoption is essential
- Underinvesting in change management relative to technology (a common 80/5 split consistently underperforms)
- Measuring activity (models deployed, training hours) instead of business outcomes
- Weakening governance in the name of speed — proportionate governance frameworks accelerate scale, they don't impede it

Appendix A — Sample AI Strategy Template

A.1 The Enterprise AI Roadmap Template

An AI roadmap is a strategic sequencing plan — a deliberate ordering of capability investments where each phase builds the data, infrastructure, and organizational readiness required for the next. The template below uses a three-horizon structure adaptable to any enterprise context.

Before completing the template, leadership should align on three things: the two or three strategic priorities AI must serve; the organization's current AI maturity level (see Chapter 10); and the total investment envelope of budget, talent, and attention available over the planning horizon.

Horizon 1: Foundation (Months 1–12) — Build the capability to build

The goal is not transformative impact but the data, infrastructure, talent, and governance without which later ambitions are structurally impossible. Key objectives include establishing a unified data platform across priority domains, deploying two to four high-value AI use cases, standing up a federated AI operating model, launching enterprise-wide AI literacy, and constituting a Model Risk Board. Illustrative early use cases include intelligent document processing, demand forecasting, customer churn prediction, and predictive maintenance.

Horizon 2: Scale (Months 13–36) — Build the capability to scale

The goal is to industrialize AI deployment — moving from isolated use cases to systematic, cross-functional programs. Key objectives include doubling models in production with deployment velocity under eight weeks, achieving 70%+ adoption, demonstrating 3x–5x portfolio ROI, and launching the first cross-domain AI integrations. Self-service tooling for business analysts and enterprise-grade model monitoring become priority infrastructure investments.

Horizon 3: Transform (Months 37–60+) — Build the capability to transform

The goal is to realize AI's full transformative potential through cross-domain intelligence, generative workflows, and new business model creation. Key objectives include deploying a unified customer intelligence layer, implementing generative AI co-creation in knowledge-intensive functions, launching at least one AI-enabled product or service, and sustaining 10%+ year-on-year learning velocity across the AI portfolio.

A.2 OKR(Objectives and Key Results) Framework for Enterprise AI Programs

OKRs provide structure for aligning AI goals across the organization and creating accountability for outcomes rather than activities. Each objective should be owned by a named executive; key results should be measurable, time-bound, and reviewed quarterly.

Horizon 1 OKRs (Year 1)

- *Establish a trusted AI foundation:* Unified data platform live by Q3; MLOps infrastructure operational by Q4; governance framework approved and zero models deployed without board sign-off by Q2.

- *Deliver measurable AI value:* Four use cases in production by Q4; combined Year 1 value exceeds target; average adoption above 65%.
- *Build organizational capability:* AI literacy training completed by 80% of people managers; federated operating model operational; deployment velocity under twelve weeks.

Horizon 2 OKRs (Years 2–3)

- *Scale AI deployment:* Fifteen or more models in production across four functions; velocity reduced to eight weeks; first cross-domain integration live.
- *Demonstrate portfolio ROI:* 3x or better AI ROA by Year 3; 8%+ year-on-year model performance improvement; AI contribution representing 15%+ of enterprise productivity gains.
- *Build capability and culture:* AI Practitioner training for 40% of relevant roles; employee AI confidence score up 20 points; full Change Acceleration playbook compliance.

Horizon 3 OKRs (Years 4–5)

- *Achieve integrated intelligence:* Unified customer intelligence layer operational; AI maturity Level 4 achieved; three or more cross-domain integrations delivering enterprise-level value.

- *Lead in AI-enabled innovation:* At least one AI-enabled revenue stream by Year 5; time-to-market for new products reduced by 40%; 12%+ learning velocity sustained.
- *Establish human-AI partnership as competitive advantage:* Generative AI workflows in three or more knowledge functions; 100% executive AI literacy; 75%+ of employees viewing AI as enabling rather than threatening.

Appendix B — Glossary

Agent / AI Agent An AI system designed to pursue goals autonomously by taking sequences of actions, using tools, and responding to the results of those actions. Unlike a model that responds to a single prompt, an agent operates over an extended horizon, making decisions about what to do next based on its current state and its objective. Enterprise AI agents are increasingly being used for complex, multi-step workflows in areas such as customer service, research synthesis, and process automation.

Agentic AI AI systems that operate with a degree of autonomy in pursuing goals — taking actions, using tools, and adapting behavior based on intermediate results without requiring human direction at each step. Agentic AI represents a significant step beyond conventional AI models that respond to individual prompts, and raises important questions about oversight, control, and accountability.

Algorithm A set of rules or instructions that a computer follows to perform a task or solve a problem. In the context of machine learning, an algorithm is the mathematical procedure used to learn patterns from data. Common ML algorithms include gradient boosting, neural networks, random forests, and linear regression. The term is sometimes used colloquially to refer to an AI model or system, though this usage conflates the algorithm (the learning procedure) with the model (the artifact produced by applying that procedure to data).

Artificial General Intelligence (AGI) A hypothetical form of AI that would have the ability to understand, learn, and apply intelligence across a wide range of tasks at a level comparable to or exceeding human capability. As of the writing of this book, AGI does not exist. The term is frequently misused in public discourse — most current AI systems, however impressive, are narrow AI, meaning they perform specific tasks well but lack the general reasoning capability that characterizes AGI.

Artificial Intelligence (AI) The broad field of computer science concerned with building systems that can perform tasks that would typically require human intelligence — including perception, reasoning, learning, planning, and natural language understanding. In enterprise contexts, AI typically refers to machine learning-based systems that learn patterns from data rather than following explicitly programmed rules.

AutoML Automated Machine Learning — tools and platforms that automate some or all of the process of selecting, training, and optimizing machine learning models. AutoML tools lower the technical barrier to building AI models, enabling data analysts and business users with limited data science expertise to develop and deploy models for specific use cases. Examples include Google AutoML, DataRobot, and H2O.ai.

Baseline Model A simple model used as a benchmark against which more sophisticated AI models are compared. A baseline might be as simple as "always predict the most common outcome" or "use last year's value as this year's forecast." Establishing a strong baseline is essential for assessing whether a more complex AI model is actually adding value.

Bias (Algorithmic) Systematic error in an AI model's outputs that results in unfair or discriminatory treatment of certain groups. Algorithmic bias can arise from biased training data (if historical data reflects past discrimination, models trained on it may perpetuate that discrimination), from flawed model design, or from the choice of what objective a model is optimized for. Addressing algorithmic bias is a central concern in responsible AI practice.

Computer Vision A field of AI focused on enabling machines to interpret and understand visual information from images and video. Enterprise applications include quality inspection in manufacturing, retail shelf monitoring, security and access control, and medical image analysis.

Data Drift The phenomenon by which the statistical properties of the data that an AI model encounters in production gradually diverge from the properties of the data on which it was trained. Data drift degrades model performance over time and is one of the primary reasons models require regular retraining. See also: Model Drift, Concept Drift.

Data Lake A centralized repository that stores large volumes of raw, unstructured, or semi-structured data in its native format until it is needed. Data lakes are a foundational infrastructure component for enterprise AI, providing a single store of historical data that can be used to train and retrain models. Distinguished from a data warehouse, which stores structured, processed data organized for specific reporting use cases.

Data Lineage The documentation of a data element's origins, transformations, and movements through an organization's systems — essentially a complete audit trail of how data was created, modified, and used. Data lineage is critical for AI governance, enabling organizations to understand where training data came from, whether it has been processed in ways that might introduce bias, and whether it meets quality and compliance requirements.

Data Mesh An organizational and architectural approach to enterprise data management that treats data as a product owned by the domain teams that generate it, rather than centralizing data ownership in a single data engineering team. The data mesh model aligns with the federated AI operating model described in this book and is increasingly being adopted by large enterprises as an alternative to centralized data lake architectures.

Data Warehouse A centralized repository of structured, processed data organized for analytical and reporting purposes. Distinguished from a data lake by its emphasis on structured, curated data and its optimization for query performance rather than raw storage capacity.

Deep Learning A subfield of machine learning that uses neural networks with many layers (hence "deep") to learn representations of data. Deep learning has produced dramatic advances in computer vision, natural language processing, and speech recognition, and underlies most modern generative AI systems.

Embeddings Mathematical representations of objects (words, documents, images, products, users) as vectors in a high-dimensional space, where objects with similar properties are positioned close together. Embeddings are a foundational technique in modern AI, enabling systems to capture semantic relationships between objects and to generalize from limited examples. They are widely used in recommendation systems, search, and natural language processing.

Explainability / Explainable AI (XAI) The degree to which the reasoning behind an AI model's output can be understood by a human. Explainability is a critical governance requirement for AI systems used in high-stakes decisions (credit, medical diagnosis, hiring), where the ability to explain why a decision was made is both ethically important and often legally required. Common techniques for improving explainability include LIME (Local Interpretable Model-Agnostic Explanations) and SHAP (SHapley Additive exPlanations).

Feature An individual measurable variable or characteristic used as an input to a machine learning model. For a customer churn model, features might include tenure in months, number of support tickets in the last 90 days, product usage frequency, and payment history. Feature selection and engineering — choosing which features to include and how to transform raw data into useful features — is one of the most important and skill-intensive aspects of building effective AI models. See also: Feature Store.

Feature Store A centralized repository of curated, versioned, and validated features that can be used across multiple AI models. Feature stores eliminate duplicated feature engineering effort, ensure consistency in how features are defined and computed, and dramatically accelerate model development by making pre-built features available to data scientists across the organization. A mature feature store is one of the most valuable infrastructure investments an enterprise AI program can make.

Fine-Tuning The process of taking a pre-trained AI model (typically a large foundation model) and training it further on domain-specific data to improve its performance on particular tasks. Fine-tuning is significantly less resource-intensive than training a model from scratch and allows enterprises to adapt general-purpose AI capabilities to their specific context without the cost of full model development.

Foundation Model A large AI model trained on a broad dataset and capable of a wide range of tasks, which can be adapted to specific applications through fine-tuning or prompting. Foundation models include large language models (LLMs) such as GPT and Claude, as well as multimodal models capable of processing both text and images. Foundation models have significantly changed the economics of enterprise AI by providing powerful general-purpose capabilities that can be customized at relatively low cost.

Generative AI AI systems capable of generating new content — text, images, audio, video, code, or other outputs — rather than simply classifying or predicting from existing data. Generative AI systems including large language models and diffusion models have demonstrated remarkable capabilities in content creation, summarization, translation, code generation, and reasoning, and are increasingly being integrated into enterprise workflows. See Chapter 12 for a discussion of generative workflows.

Ground Truth The actual, verified outcome against which an AI model's predictions are compared to measure its accuracy. For a churn prediction model, ground truth is whether each customer actually churned within the prediction window. Establishing clean, reliable ground truth is essential for both training and evaluating AI models, and is often significantly more difficult in practice than building the model itself.

Hallucination The phenomenon by which a generative AI model produces outputs that are plausible-sounding but factually incorrect, fabricated, or nonsensical. Hallucination is a significant limitation of current large language models and a key consideration in enterprise AI deployment, particularly for use cases where factual accuracy is critical. Mitigation strategies include retrieval-augmented generation (RAG), grounding outputs in verified sources, and human review processes.

Human-in-the-Loop (HITL) An AI deployment approach in which human judgment is incorporated into the AI decision process — either by having humans review and approve AI recommendations before they are acted upon, or by providing feedback on AI outputs that is used to improve the model. The degree of human involvement varies by use case: for high-stakes, low-frequency decisions, full human review may be appropriate; for high-frequency, lower-stakes decisions, statistical sampling of human review may be sufficient.

Inference The process of using a trained AI model to generate predictions or outputs from new input data. Distinguished from training, which is the process of building the model. In production AI systems, inference happens continuously as the model processes real-world inputs. Inference latency — the time required to generate an output — is a critical performance consideration for real-time AI applications.

Large Language Model (LLM) A type of foundation model trained on large volumes of text data, capable of generating, summarizing, translating, and reasoning about language. LLMs such as GPT-4, Claude, and Llama underlie most current generative AI applications and are increasingly being deployed in enterprise contexts for tasks including document analysis, customer service, code generation, and knowledge management.

Latency The time delay between an input being provided to an AI system and the output being returned. Latency is a critical performance dimension for real-time AI applications — a fraud detection system that takes five seconds to score a transaction is useless for online payment fraud prevention. Low-latency AI inference typically requires specialized hardware and infrastructure optimization.

Learning Velocity The rate at which an AI system or AI program improves its performance over time through accumulated learning from production data. Learning velocity is introduced in Chapter 11 as a key strategic metric for AI-driven enterprises — an indicator not just of current AI performance but of the organization's capability to improve continuously. See also: AI Flywheel.

Machine Learning (ML) A subfield of artificial intelligence in which systems learn patterns from data rather than following explicitly programmed rules. Machine learning encompasses a range of techniques including supervised learning (learning from labeled examples), unsupervised learning (finding patterns in unlabeled data), and reinforcement learning (learning through trial and error). Most enterprise AI applications are built on machine learning techniques.

MLOps (Machine Learning Operations) The set of practices, tools, and cultural norms that apply DevOps principles to the machine learning lifecycle — enabling organizations to build, deploy, monitor, and improve AI models reliably and at scale. MLOps addresses the industrialization of AI, transforming model development from a bespoke artisanal activity into a repeatable operational process. Core MLOps capabilities include automated training pipelines, model registries, deployment automation, and production monitoring. See Chapter 10 for a detailed discussion.

Model Drift The degradation of an AI model's performance over time as the relationship between input variables and the target outcome changes. Model drift is caused by changes in the real world — shifting customer behavior, evolving market conditions, changes in operational processes — that make a model's training data an increasingly poor representation of current reality. Regular model monitoring and retraining is required to manage model drift. See also: Data Drift, Concept Drift.

Model Risk The risk of adverse outcomes resulting from decisions made based on incorrect or misused AI models. Model risk includes errors in model development (using the wrong algorithm or training data), model implementation (deploying a model in a context it was not designed for), and model use (relying on model outputs in ways that exceed their reliability). Model risk management — a well-established discipline in financial services — is increasingly being adopted across industries as AI systems take on more consequential decision roles.

Natural Language Processing (NLP) A field of AI focused on enabling machines to understand, interpret, and generate human language. NLP powers applications including document analysis, sentiment analysis, conversational AI, translation, and content generation. Large language models represent the current state of the art in NLP.

Neural Network A machine learning architecture inspired by the structure of the human brain, consisting of layers of interconnected nodes (neurons) that learn to recognize patterns in data through repeated exposure to examples. Neural networks are the foundation of deep learning and underlie most modern AI capabilities including computer vision, natural language processing, and generative AI.

Overfitting A common failure mode in machine learning in which a model learns the specific patterns in its training data so thoroughly that it fails to generalize to new, unseen data. An overfitted model performs well on the data it was trained on but poorly on real-world data. Overfitting is particularly common when models are complex relative to the amount of training data available.

Prompt Engineering The practice of designing and optimizing the inputs (prompts) provided to a large language model to achieve desired outputs. Effective prompt engineering can dramatically improve the quality, consistency, and reliability of LLM outputs without requiring model fine-tuning. It is an emerging professional skill of significant value in enterprise LLM deployment.

RAG (Retrieval-Augmented Generation) A technique that improves the accuracy and reliability of large language model outputs by supplementing the model's internal knowledge with information retrieved from a curated external knowledge base at inference time. RAG is widely used in enterprise AI applications to reduce hallucination, ensure outputs are grounded in current and accurate information, and adapt general-purpose LLMs to specific organizational knowledge contexts.

Reinforcement Learning from Human Feedback (RLHF) A training technique used to align large language models with human preferences by having human raters evaluate model outputs and using those ratings to further train the model. RLHF is one of the key techniques that has made modern LLMs more helpful, harmless, and honest.

Responsible AI The practice of designing, building, and deploying AI systems in ways that are safe, fair, transparent, accountable, and aligned with human values. Responsible AI encompasses algorithmic fairness, explainability, privacy protection, security, and governance — ensuring that AI systems generate value without causing harm to individuals, communities, or society

Supervised Learning A machine learning approach in which a model is trained on labeled examples — data points for which the correct output is known — to learn the relationship between inputs and outputs. Most enterprise predictive AI applications (churn prediction, demand forecasting, fraud detection) use supervised learning. The quality and representativeness of the labeled training data is the single most important determinant of supervised learning model performance.

Transfer Learning A machine learning technique in which a model trained on one task is adapted to perform a different but related task, leveraging the knowledge gained during the original training. Transfer learning dramatically reduces the data and compute required to build capable models for specific enterprise use cases by starting from the rich representations learned by large foundation models trained on vast datasets.

Transformer A neural network architecture introduced in 2017 that has become the dominant paradigm for large language models and many other state-of-the-art AI systems. The transformer architecture enables models to learn complex relationships between elements of a sequence (such as words in a sentence) through a mechanism called attention, which allows the model to weigh the relevance of different parts of the input when generating each part of the output.

Unsupervised Learning A machine learning approach in which a model learns patterns in data without labeled examples, identifying structure and relationships that are not explicitly specified. Common unsupervised learning techniques include clustering (grouping similar data points), dimensionality reduction (representing high-dimensional data in lower-dimensional form), and anomaly detection (identifying data points that deviate from normal patterns).

Appendix C — AI Tools Landscape for Enterprises

The enterprise AI tools landscape is large and rapidly evolving. This appendix maps key tool categories across the AI value chain — from data to model to deployment to governance. Tool selection depends heavily on your existing stack, cloud relationships, team capabilities, and use cases. Treat this as a map of the territory, not a procurement checklist.

C.1 Data Infrastructure

Cloud Data Platforms

- **Snowflake** — Market-leading cloud data warehouse; strong SQL analytics and broad ecosystem integration
- **Databricks** — Unified data and AI platform built on Spark; ideal for large-scale model training and complex transformations
- **Google BigQuery** — Serverless warehouse tightly integrated with Google Cloud AI; cost-effective for variable workloads
- **Amazon Redshift** — AWS-native data warehouse; natural fit for organizations already on AWS
- **Microsoft Fabric** — Unified analytics platform integrating data engineering, warehousing, and BI; strong Microsoft 365 and Azure ML integration

Data Integration & ETL

- **Fivetran** — Automated pipelines with pre-built connectors to hundreds of SaaS and database sources

- **dbt** — SQL-based transformation framework; the standard for analytics engineering with version control built in
- **Apache Kafka** — Distributed event streaming for real-time data ingestion pipelines
- **Informatica** — Enterprise-grade integration with strong data quality and governance; widely used in regulated industries

Data Quality & Observability

- **Monte Carlo** — Monitors pipelines for anomalies, schema changes, and freshness issues
- **Great Expectations** — Open-source framework for defining and enforcing data quality as code
- **Atlan** — Data catalog combining discovery, lineage tracking, and governance workflows

C.2 Vector Databases & Embedding Infrastructure

Vector Databases

- **Pinecone** — Fully managed vector database; leading choice for production RAG and semantic search applications; strong performance at scale
- **Weaviate** — Open-source vector database with hybrid search (vector + keyword); strong multimodal support and GraphQL interface
- **Qdrant** — Open-source, high-performance vector database with rich filtering capabilities; well-suited for complex similarity search use cases

- **Chroma** — Lightweight open-source vector store popular for prototyping and smaller-scale LLM applications
- **Milvus** — Open-source, cloud-native vector database built for billion-scale similarity search; widely used in enterprise deployments
- **pgvector** — PostgreSQL extension adding vector similarity search; ideal for organizations wanting vector search without a separate database system
- **Azure AI Search** — Microsoft's managed search service with native vector search and hybrid retrieval; integrates tightly with Azure OpenAI

Embedding Models

- **OpenAI Embeddings (text-embedding-3)** — Most widely used embedding model for enterprise RAG pipelines; strong general-purpose performance
- **Cohere Embed** — Enterprise-focused embedding model with strong multilingual support and retrieval optimization
- **Sentence Transformers** — Open-source library of pre-trained embedding models; widely used for on-premise and cost-sensitive deployments

C.3 Machine Learning Development

Development Environments & IDEs

- **Jupyter Notebooks / JupyterLab** — De facto standard for interactive model development; a development tool, not a deployment tool

- **VS Code with Python** — Full-featured ML engineering environment with strong AI extension support including GitHub Copilot and Pylance
- **PyCharm** — JetBrains IDE with strong Python and data science tooling; popular in enterprise engineering teams
- **Google Colab** — Cloud-hosted Jupyter environment with free GPU access; widely used for experimentation and collaboration
- **Deepnote** — Collaborative cloud notebook with real-time co-editing and built-in data integrations; suited for team-based data science
- **Weights & Biases (W&B)** — Experiment tracking and model visualization; essential for managing iterative development complexity

AutoML & Low-Code ML

- **DataRobot** — Enterprise AutoML with strong explainability and monitoring; suited for business-oriented data scientists
- **H2O.ai** — Open-source and enterprise AutoML with strong tabular data performance
- **Google Vertex AI AutoML** — Managed AutoML tightly integrated with BigQuery and Google Cloud

Feature Stores

- **Feast** — Open-source, widely adopted, well-integrated with major cloud platforms
- **Tecton** — Enterprise platform with strong real-time feature computation; suited for low-latency applications

- **Databricks Feature Store** — Native to Databricks; natural choice for organizations already on that platform

C.4 Vibe Coding & AI-Assisted Development

Vibe coding tools allow developers — and increasingly non-developers — to build software through natural language instructions, AI pair programming, and prompt-driven code generation. This category is evolving rapidly and is becoming a standard part of enterprise developer toolchains.

AI Code Editors & IDEs

- **Cursor** — AI-first code editor built on VS Code; supports natural language code generation, multi-file editing, and codebase-aware chat; leading choice for AI-native development workflows
- **Windsurf (by Codeium)** — AI code editor with agentic capabilities; strong context awareness across large codebases; competitive alternative to Cursor
- **GitHub Copilot** — Microsoft's AI pair programmer integrated into VS Code, JetBrains, and other IDEs; the most widely deployed AI coding assistant in enterprise environments
- **JetBrains AI Assistant** — AI coding capabilities natively integrated across the JetBrains IDE family (IntelliJ, PyCharm, WebStorm); strong for Java and Python enterprise teams
- **Amazon CodeWhisperer** — AWS's AI code companion with strong security scanning and AWS API awareness; natural fit for AWS-native development teams

Agentic Coding & Autonomous Development

- **Claude Code** — Anthropic's terminal-based agentic coding tool; capable of reading, writing, and executing code across entire codebases with multi-step reasoning; strong for complex engineering tasks
- **OpenAI Codex / ChatGPT with Code Interpreter** — Code generation and execution environment; widely used for data analysis, scripting, and prototyping tasks
- **Devin (by Cognition)** — Autonomous AI software engineer capable of end-to-end task completion including environment setup, debugging, and deployment; early-stage but significant for longer-horizon automation
- **SWE-agent** — Open-source autonomous coding agent from Princeton; designed to solve real GitHub issues; useful for research and internal tooling contexts

No-Code / Low-Code App Building

- **Bolt.new** — Browser-based AI app builder; generates full-stack applications from natural language prompts; strong for rapid prototyping and internal tools
- **Lovable** — AI-powered web app builder focused on product and design quality; generates deployable React applications from conversational prompts
- **v0 (by Vercel)** — AI UI component generator producing production-ready React and Tailwind code from text and image prompts; widely used by frontend teams

- **Replit Agent** — Cloud-based coding environment with an AI agent that can build, run, and deploy applications from natural language; accessible to non-developers
- **Retool AI** — Low-code internal tool builder with integrated LLM capabilities; strong for enterprises building AI-powered internal applications on top of existing databases and APIs

C.5 MLOps & Model Lifecycle Management

End-to-End MLOps Platforms

- **MLflow** — Open-source; covers experiment tracking, model registry, and deployment; widely adopted across cloud platforms
- **Kubeflow** — Kubernetes-native ML workflows; highly flexible but operationally complex
- **Amazon SageMaker** — Comprehensive managed ML platform covering labeling, training, deployment, and monitoring; AWS-native
- **Azure Machine Learning** — Managed platform with strong Azure data service and enterprise identity integration
- **Google Vertex AI** — Google's managed AI platform supporting both custom models and foundation model deployment

Model Monitoring

- **Evidently AI** — Open-source; strong data drift detection and performance tracking
- **Arize AI** — Enterprise observability covering both traditional ML and LLM monitoring

- **WhyLabs** — AI observability with particular strength in monitoring LLM outputs in production

C.6 Generative AI & LLM Tools

Foundation Model Access

- **OpenAI API** — Access to GPT-4o and o-series models; dominant in enterprise generative AI with broad ecosystem support
- **Anthropic Claude** — Strong on reasoning, analysis, and long-context tasks; growing enterprise adoption for nuanced judgment and agentic use cases
- **Azure OpenAI Service** — Enterprise-grade OpenAI model access via Azure with strong privacy, compliance, and Microsoft 365 integration
- **Google Gemini** — Frontier multimodal model family with deep Google Workspace and Cloud integration
- **AWS Bedrock** — Unified API access to multiple foundation models (Claude, Llama, Mistral, and others); ideal for AWS-native organizations wanting model flexibility
- **Meta Llama** — Leading open-weight model family; widely used for on-premise and private cloud deployments where data cannot leave the enterprise environment
- **Mistral AI** — European open-weight and API model provider; strong performance-to-cost ratio; increasingly adopted in privacy-sensitive European enterprise contexts

LLM Application Development

- **LangChain** — Open-source framework for building LLM applications; strong agent, RAG, and chain-of-thought workflow support
- **LlamaIndex** — Data framework for RAG applications connecting LLMs to enterprise knowledge bases; widely used for document intelligence
- **Haystack** — Open-source NLP framework with strong support for enterprise search and question-answering systems
- **Semantic Kernel** — Microsoft's open-source SDK for integrating LLMs into enterprise applications; strong .NET and C# support; suited for Microsoft-centric development teams

LLM Observability & Evaluation

- **LangSmith** — LangChain's platform for tracing, testing, and monitoring LLM applications in production
- **Helicone** — Open-source LLM observability platform; logs, monitors, and analyzes API usage across all major model providers
- **Promptfoo** — Open-source LLM evaluation and red-teaming tool; enables systematic testing of prompts and model outputs before deployment
- **Braintrust** — Enterprise LLM evaluation platform with dataset management, scoring, and CI/CD integration for prompt pipelines

C.7 Enterprise AI Platforms & Copilots

Horizontal Enterprise AI Platforms

- **Microsoft Copilot for M365** — AI assistant integrated into Word, Excel, Outlook, and Teams; default entry point for generative AI in Microsoft-centric enterprises
- **Microsoft Azure AI Studio** — Unified platform for building, evaluating, and deploying enterprise AI applications on Azure; supports RAG, fine-tuning, and agent development
- **Google Workspace AI (Gemini for Workspace)** — AI capabilities across Gmail, Docs, Sheets, and Meet; natural fit for Google Workspace enterprises
- **Salesforce Einstein** — Generative AI integrated throughout the Salesforce CRM platform including Sales Cloud, Service Cloud, and Marketing Cloud
- **ServiceNow AI** — AI for IT service management, HR workflows, and enterprise process automation
- **Glean** — Enterprise AI search and knowledge management indexing content across an organization's full application ecosystem
- **Notion AI** — AI writing and knowledge management integrated into Notion workspaces; popular in technology and product teams

Vertical & Specialized Enterprise AI

- **Harvey** — AI platform purpose-built for legal workflows including contract review, due diligence, and legal research; widely adopted in law firms and in-house legal teams
- **Abridge** — AI-powered clinical documentation platform that generates medical notes from patient-physician conversations; deployed in major health systems

- **Ironclad AI** — AI-powered contract lifecycle management; automates contract review, negotiation, and obligation tracking
- **Moveworks** — Enterprise AI platform for IT and HR service automation; uses LLMs to resolve employee requests through natural language
- **Writer** — Enterprise generative AI platform with strong brand voice control, compliance guardrails, and workflow integration; suited for content-heavy organizations

C.8 AI Governance & Responsible AI

Model Explainability

- **SHAP** — Most widely adopted explainability technique; provides global and local prediction explanations; available as open-source Python library
- **LIME** — Model-agnostic local explainability; useful for explaining individual predictions of complex models
- **IBM AI Explainability 360** — Open-source toolkit offering a range of explainability methods and metrics

AI Risk & Governance

- **IBM OpenScale** — Enterprise AI monitoring with strong bias detection and model risk management for regulated industries
- **Holistic AI** — Covers risk assessment, bias auditing, and compliance monitoring across the AI portfolio
- **Credo AI** — Focused on policy management, risk assessment, and compliance documentation for enterprise deployments

- **Fairly AI** — Automated bias testing and fairness monitoring platform; designed for financial services and HR AI applications in regulated environments

Data Privacy & Security

- **Privacera** — Unified data access governance for managing privacy controls across cloud environments used in AI training
- **BigID** — Discovers, classifies, and manages sensitive data used in AI systems
- **Nightfall AI** — DLP (Data Loss Prevention) platform with LLM-aware detection; prevents sensitive data from being inadvertently sent to external AI models

Appendix D — Sample AI use cases

A quick-reference guide to the highest-value AI applications across major enterprise functions.

D.1 Finance & Accounting

- Intelligent accounts payable automation — invoice processing, three-way matching, payment scheduling
- Automated financial close — journal entry automation, reconciliation, anomaly detection
- Cash flow forecasting and liquidity optimization
- Fraud detection and financial crime surveillance
- Natural language querying of financial data and automated variance analysis
- Tax compliance monitoring and audit support

D.2 Supply Chain & Operations

- Demand forecasting at SKU, location, and channel level
- Inventory optimization and replenishment automation
- Predictive maintenance for production equipment and fleet
- Supplier risk scoring and supply disruption prediction
- Dynamic logistics routing and network optimization
- Quality inspection and defect detection via computer vision

D.3 Sales & Commercial

- Sales opportunity scoring and pipeline prioritization

- Next-best-action recommendations for sales representatives
- Pricing optimization and discount approval automation
- Churn prediction and account health scoring
- Deal win/loss analysis and competitive intelligence
- Sales performance analytics and coaching recommendations

D.4 Marketing

- Customer segmentation and propensity modeling (purchase, churn, upgrade)
- Personalization at scale — content, offers, timing, and channel
- Marketing mix modeling and budget optimization
- Customer lifetime value modeling
- AI-assisted content generation and creative testing
- Multi-touch attribution modeling across channels

D.5 Human Resources & People Analytics

- Talent acquisition optimization — resume screening, candidate scoring
- Employee attrition prediction and retention intervention
- Workforce planning and skills gap analysis
- Personalized learning and development recommendations
- Compensation benchmarking and pay equity analysis
- Internal mobility matching — connecting employees to open opportunities

D.6 Customer Service & Experience

- Intelligent routing and triage across channels

- Conversational AI and self-service automation
- Agent assist — real-time knowledge surfacing and next-best-action during live interactions
- Sentiment analysis and conversation quality scoring
- Complaint pattern detection and root cause analysis
- Voice of customer synthesis from unstructured feedback at scale

D.7 Information Technology & Cybersecurity

- AIOps — anomaly detection, root cause analysis, automated remediation
- Cybersecurity threat detection and behavioral analytics
- Automated vulnerability assessment and patch prioritization
- IT service desk automation and intelligent ticket routing
- Infrastructure capacity planning and optimization
- AI-assisted code generation, code review, and test automation

D.8 Research & Product Development

- Literature and prior art synthesis across large document corpora
- Molecule and materials discovery via generative models
- Simulation and digital twin optimization for accelerated product testing
- Customer insight synthesis from unstructured feedback
- Competitive product and patent intelligence monitoring
- Generative design for product concept generation and optimization

My bookshelf

- AI For Business: A Practical Guide For Business Leaders to Extract Value From Artificial Intelligence by Peter Verster
- Co-Intelligence: Living and Working with AI Paperback by Ethan Mollick
- Empire of AI: Inside the reckless race for total domination by Karen Hao
- Supremacy:AI, ChatGPT and the race that is changing the world by Parmy Olson
- AI Valley : Microsoft, Google, and the Trillion-Dollar Race to Cash In on Artificial Intelligence by Gary Rivlin
- The AI-Driven Leader: Harnessing AI to Make Faster, Smarter Decisions by Geoff Woods
- The Shortest History of AI by Toby Walsh
- The Co-Intelligence Revolution: How Humans and AI Co-Create New Value by Professor Venkat Ramaswamy , Dr Krishnan Narayanan
- AI First: The Playbook for a Future-Proof Business and Brand by Adam Brotman , Andy Sack
- Human Edge in the AI Age: Eight Timeless Mantras for Success by Nitin Seth

- AI Value Creators: Beyond the Generative AI User Mindset by Rob Thomas , Paul Zikopoulos , et al.
- Generative AI: The Insights You Need from Harvard Business Review by Harvard Business Review , Ethan Mollick, et al.

Other books by the same author

- Neural Networks with R
- Understanding Growth Marketing
- Advanced Prompt Engineering for LLMs
- Applied RAG - Practical Retrieval Augmented Generation with Python
- Advanced AI: Neural Networks and Deep Learning
- Generative AI: Concepts, Tools and Applications
- Principles of Artificial Intelligence, Machine Learning and Large Language Models
- Foundations of Natural Language Processing
- IoT Security, Data Management and Cloud Integration
- Understanding Supply Chain Analytics
- Inventory Optimization using AI
- AI Startup Guide Fundraising & Valuation
- AI-preneurship

About the book

Winning with AI is a practical playbook for enterprise leaders looking to move beyond AI experimentation and build a sustainable, value-driven AI capability.

The book begins by establishing that AI strategy must start with business outcomes, not technology. It walks through assessing organizational AI maturity, building an AI-first mindset, and laying the data and digital foundations that make AI possible. The core of the book covers designing an AI strategy around eight pillars — vision, business value, operating model, funding, data platforms, risk, literacy, and change management. It then addresses the organizational machinery needed to execute: the right operating model (federated being the recommended approach), the AI Centre of Excellence, key roles like the CAIO and AI translators, and governance structures spanning strategy, operations, and ethics. Architecture, people capability, and AI fluency are covered in depth, emphasizing that technology alone never drives transformation — people do.

The book also tackles responsible AI, measurement frameworks, and lifecycle governance, arguing that ethics and governance accelerate scale rather than impede it.

It closes with industry best practices and common mistakes, distilling everything into a clear message: **start with business problems, build solid foundations, govern proportionately, invest in people, and treat AI as a compounding organizational asset — not a one-time project.**

www.ingramcontent.com/pod-product-compliance
Lightning Source LLC
LaVergne TN
LVHW022217200926
848481LV00006B/1997
9798903928781